MURDER MYSTERIES VOL 1

Ideal for interactive team performances. Scripts can also be
personalised for groups of people.

The way the plays are performed is simple. A murder is
committed, actors interrogate suspects, the murderer is
unmasked.

All guests have to do is guess the murderer's identity and work
out how the killing occurred.

Oh, and they also have to cast themselves as suspects, reading
from prepared scripts!

For performance rights contact www.johndunneplays.com.

PHOENIX PRODUCTIONS PRESENTS

DRAMATIC
MURDER MYSTERY

MURDER, MYSTERY AND MAYHEM

Phone: 01420 472664
Email: info@phoenixarts.co.uk

Artwork: The Studio - 01420 473981

DRAMATIC MURDER MYSTERY

By

John Dunne

Characters
Lady Etherington-Smythe
Inspector Michaels
Sheila
Patrick
Dennis
Carol
Louise
Malcolm
Sergeant

Lady Etherington-Smythe has been brutally murdered. A village hall full of actors, one of whom is the murderer. Can Inspector Michaels solve the mystery before others meet their maker?

ONE

ENTER LADY ETHERINGTON-SMYTHE FOLLOWED BY PATRICK

SMYTHE. Patrick?

PATRICK. Yes, Lady Etherington.

SMYTHE. Patrick. If I've told you once, I've told you a thousand times.

PATRICK. Yes, Lady Etherington.

SMYTHE. Either address me as Your Ladyship, or Lady Etherington-Smythe. Not – and I repeat, not – Lady Etherington or Lady Smythe. I have a double-barrelled name and both barrels should be discharged at the same time. Do I make myself clear?

PATRICK. Yes, Your Ladyship.

SMYTHE. Now, where are the performers?

PATRICK. There appears to be a muck up with the bookings.

SMYTHE. But I handle the bookings, Patrick.

PATRICK. I know.

SMYTHE. So who do we have this evening?

PATRICK. I'm not sure. Nobody seems to have arrived.

SMYTHE. But it's gone seven.

PATRICK. I know.

SMYTHE. Well, I can't wait forever. You had better go and fetch my car. I'll hold the fort.

PATRICK. As you wish.

PATRICK EXITS

LADY SMYTHE ADDRESSES THE AUDIENCE

SMYTHE. I have to attend a presentation this evening. Camden Council are honouring my husband and I really must be there. *(She fishes into her bag)* Well, I suppose while I'm here, I might as well keep you good people occupied. Perhaps I might say a few words. It's my husband who should be addressing you really. After all he is the chairman of trustees who run this place.

(She unfolds a sheet of paper) Anyway, on to business. I'd like to start by welcoming everybody here tonight and to offer my special thanks to those of you who were involved in last week's jumble sale.

(She smiles) I expect you will be eager to learn how much was raised at this exciting event. *(She pauses for effect)* I can tell you that we raised a staggering £32.15p. *(She pauses for applause)* And when we add all this to the magnificent amount acquired from the proceeds of Mrs O'Brien's milk bottle top campaign – all this will naturally be sent forthwith to the Blind Dogs for the Guides.

(She then glares at the audience) And the person who put in a two euro coin ought to be ashamed of themselves! They were obviously French or German - or both!

(She refers to her notes) But never mind all that. We'll soon be shot of those pecky Europeans. That aside, I bet you would like to know the programme for this weeks' Spring Fair

On Monday we have the Spring Fair itself. There will be a jam stand, tombola, roll-a-penny, maypole dancing, cakes – courtesy of the Day Centre – plants and flowers, old books and of course, our very own White Elephant stand.

Tuesday will see our sponsored knit. Entry forms must be in as soon as possible for this worthwhile activity – knitting blankets for the elderly - poor dears.

Wednesday is the playgroup barbecue evening. If wet, the barbecue will be held inside the hall.

And Thursday is our Spring Gala concert. I'm especially looking forward to this one. *(She dashes over to a member of the audience)* Terry here will play songs on his new Yamaha electric organ. An evening of entertainment not to be missed.

ENTER PATRICK

PATRICK. Your Ladyship.

SMYTHE. What is it? Can't you see I'm busy? *(She continues)* And as for Friday, there is a special tea-dance event for the younger people in our community. This is designed to keep them away from knives and forks and anything else that may cause concern. *(peers into the audience)* And yes, there <u>will</u> be a dress code. No hoods - and jeans should be worn over the hips and not around the nether regions!

PATRICK. Your Ladyship. I think the performers are beginning to arrive.

SMYTHE. And not before time. *(She addresses the audience)* At last, ladies and gentlemen, I have pleasure in presenting – Queen's Crescent Drama Group – better known as Scribes and Thespians – but we don't judge peoples' sexual preferences! *(To PATRICK)* Now that's sorted, I really do need to get on.

PATRICK. Aren't you going to welcome them?

SMYTHE. Oh no, you can do that. I'm far too busy.

SHE EXITS

PATRICK. *(to the audience)* She's not really a lady, you know. Her first husband was something high up in the civil service. Was made an MFI or something. Her Ladyship then got it into her head that she was royalty itself. The problem is her second husband - Jack Smith, a builder from Essex and chairman of this centre - puts money into this place so we all have to humour the old bat. The only reason she's in charge around here is because Jack built the extension at cost and the committee felt obliged to put her in charge as a recognition bla, bla, bla.

She even changed her married name from Smith to Smythe and double-barrelled it with her first husband's name. I ask you, *(mimicking)* "Etherington Smythe is a double-barrelled name and both barrels should be discharged at the same time." I'll discharge 'em – with pleasure. I think it's about time Jack sorted her out - she's making a donkey's arse out of him. There's even talk of her having a fancy man in tow, but I'm not one to gossip.

And as for me, I actually run the place, despite what she says. I'm the "domiciliary facilities manager" and it's time we got on with the show.

HE EXITS

Murder Mysteries Vol 1

ENTER SHEILA

SHEILA. *(Looks at the audience)* Oh my God! *(Calls off stage)* Dennis! The audience are here. This is dreadful! This simply isn't happening to me. *(To the audience)* I'm so sorry. You've all arrived far too early. Can't you go back into the bar and get another drink or something? Where on earth is that husband of mine? Dennis?

ENTER DENNIS

DENNIS. Yes, Sheila. What do you want?

SHEILA. Dennis, there you are. What have you been doing?

DENNIS. I was just unloading the car.

SHEILA. Forget about the car. As you can see, the audience has arrived.

DENNIS. But they can't have.

SHEILA. Look for yourself if you don't believe me.

DENNIS. *(Looks at the audience)* Oh my God, how long have they been here?

SHEILA. By the look of them, they've been here since the dawn of time.

DENNIS. There's nothing to worry about.

SHEILA. We're just about to start a play and you say there's nothing to worry about.

DENNIS. *(Addressing the audience)* I'm sorry about this, ladies and gentlemen. A slight upset.

SHEILA. And where are the others?

DENNIS. I saw Carol in the car park.

SHEILA. Oh, yes! Carol!

DENNIS. Shall I go and fetch her?

SHEILA. No, you will not go and fetch her. I'll sort it all out – I generally do.

DENNIS. That's not fair.

SHEILA. I don't suppose it is. Now, where is that Carol?

DENNIS EXITS

ENTER CAROL

CAROL. What's going on, Sheila?

SHEILA. As you can see, the audience have arrived early.

CAROL. I think you'll find we're late.

SHEILA. *(To the audience)* I really must apologise for the delay, ladies and gentlemen. If you'll just give us a few seconds to gather our thoughts.

CAROL. Where are the others, Sheila?

SHEILA. I don't know, do I? Have you seen Louise and Malcolm?

CAROL. No.

SHEILA. Louise should be here. After all, she took the booking.

CAROL. Shall I go and find her?

SHEILA. Please, if you would.

CAROL. Is Louise for the high jump, Sheila?

SHEILA. Just go and find her, will you? And don't take all night about it. We do have a show to perform.

CAROL. That's more than we had this afternoon.

SHEILA. Teething troubles, that was all.

CAROL. We're supposed to be performing a drama this evening – not a farce.

SHEILA. Will you get on, please?

CAROL. I'm going, I'm going.

SHEILA. Hopefully without any of your snide remarks.

CAROL. What's that supposed to mean?

SHEILA. Nothing. Louise!

CAROL EXITS

ENTER LOUISE

LOUISE. What are all these people doing here, Sheila?

SHEILA. I could well ask you the same question, Louise.

LOUISE. I don't understand.

SHEILA. Somebody got the booking wrong.

LOUISE. No, I didn't!

SHEILA. Where are the others? Where's Malcolm?

LOUISE. He's parking the car.

SHEILA. Typical!

LOUISE. Sheila, I didn't get the booking wrong, honest!

SHEILA. Well, somebody did, Louise. And you're supposed to be the production manager of this company.

LOUISE. I know I didn't get it wrong. And I can prove it. I've got the confirmation form in the car.

SHEILA. Never mind all that now. We're here and that's all that counts.

LOUISE. So what happens now?

SHEILA. I don't know, do I?

LOUISE. Whatever we do, we'd better do it quick. The audience is getting restless.

SHEILA. Louise, will you go and find Carol? I want another word with her.

LOUISE. I'll try and find that confirmation form as well.

SHEILA. Forget about the form. Find Carol for me.

LOUISE. Okay, okay. I'm going.

LOUISE EXITS

ENTER CAROL

CAROL. Sheila, I've got an idea.

SHEILA. Have you now?

CAROL. We're obviously in a bit of a pickle.

SHEILA. How very observant of you.

CAROL. Why don't we improvise until the others get here?

SHEILA. Improvise?

CAROL. It'll save us standing around looking gormless.

SHEILA. Who's looking gormless?

CAROL. I didn't mean –

SHEILA. Are you saying I look gormless?

CAROL. No, of course not.

SHEILA. We can't just improvise.

CAROL. Why not? We're actors, aren't we? Quick on our feet, and all that.

SHEILA. The audience rather expect a play, Carol.

CAROL. So, what do we do?

SHEILA. We do what we always do.

CAROL. What, panic?

SHEILA. We get on with our programme as best we can. *(Turns to the audience)* Ladies and gentlemen. As you've no doubt gathered, you – we – appear to have miscalculated the timing of this evening's performance. A slight administrative error.

CAROL. It wasn't Louise's fault.

SHEILA. I'm not saying it was her fault. So stop going on about it.

CAROL. Right, I'm off to find the others.

SHEILA. If you see Louise, could I have another word?

CAROL EXITS

ENTER LOUISE

SHEILA. *(To the audience)* So if you would just bear with us for a moment – while we regroup our thoughts, as it were – we will start as soon as possible. Just as soon as the other actors arrive, in fact.

LOUISE. I still can't find my confirmation form.

SHEILA. Never mind about that. Who's arrived exactly?

LOUISE. I'm not sure.

SHEILA. Where on earth is everyone?

LOUISE. I expect they went home after this afternoon's rehearsal.

SHEILA. Went home?

LOUISE. It was late. People have to eat.

SHEILA. This is disastrous. I really must have a word with this Smith woman.

LOUISE. Smythe. Lady Etherington-Smythe. Her name is Lady Etherington-Smythe.

SHEILA. Thank you, Louise. I know <u>exactly</u> who she is. If only you paid as much detail to the bookings as you do to peoples' names.

LOUISE. That wasn't my fault. I told you.

SHEILA. It's hardly relevant now, Louise. This is an important booking for us and we're screwing it up like tissue paper. Lady Etherington-Smythe will never ask us back, you know. We were going to make a killing here.

LOUISE. We'll just have to make do with a wounding.

SHEILA. Very funny, Louise. Except I'm not amused.

LOUISE. You're not, are you?

SHEILA. No.

LOUISE. I know where I've left the confirmation form. In the boot of my car. Won't be a sec.

SHEILA. Before you go, find Carol for me. I need to speak to her again.

LOUISE EXITS

ENTER CAROL

SHEILA. Carol.

CAROL. Yes, Sheila.

SHEILA. Do you have a second?

CAROL. Oh dear, Sheila. You have that cross look.

SHEILA. It's about that dress.

CAROL. What about my dress?

SHEILA. You're not wearing that dress during the show, are you?

CAROL. I thought I might, yes.

SHEILA. It's rather – what can I say?

CAROL. You can say what you like. I'm still wearing this dress.

SHEILA. It doesn't leave much to the imagination, does it?

CAROL. I don't believe you, Sheila. Here we are, over an hour late for a performance and you're worried about my dress.

SHEILA. I haven't got time for this. I must speak to Lady Smith -

CAROL. Lady Etherington-Smythe.

SHEILA. I know what her name is. I took the booking, remember?

CAROL. Then maybe <u>you</u> got the wrong information.

SHEILA. I did not get the wrong information. I took the booking and passed it on to Louise to finish off the final details.

CAROL. I'll fetch Louise for you.

SHEILA. You do that. Oh, and Carol.

CAROL. Yes?

SHEILA. Don't challenge me like that again.

CAROL. I wasn't challenging anyone, Sheila.

CAROL EXITS

ENTER LADY ETHERINGTON-SMYTHE

SHEILA. Ah, Lady Smith.

SMYTHE. If I've told you once, I've told you a thousand times. Either address me as Your Ladyship, or Lady Etherington-Smythe. Not – and I repeat, not – Lady Etherington or Lady Smythe – or Lady Smith. I have a double-barrelled name and both barrels should be discharged at the same time. Do I make myself clear?

SHEILA. Yes, Your Ladyship.

SMYTHE. So, have your acting people arrived?

SHEILA. I'm afraid not.

SMYTHE. But it's gone eight.

SHEILA. I know.

SMYTHE. They should be here by now. I distinctly said –

SHEILA. I know.

SMYTHE. So, where are they?

SHEILA. I don't know.

SMYTHE. Well, I can't wait forever. I have to attend a presentation this evening. The Chamber of Commerce is honouring my husband, Lord Etherington-Smythe. I really must be there.

SHEILA. I'm so sorry, Lady Etherington-Smythe. Whatever must you think of us? I really must apologise for the delay.

SMYTHE. It can't be helped, I suppose. People here are so patient. They're used to having to wait.

SHEILA. That's all right, then.

SMYTHE. As for myself, I must love you and leave you. So please, have a super evening. And do say hello and goodbye to your fellow actors for me – when they finally turn up. I must dash.

LADY SMYTHE EXITS

ENTER DENNIS

SHEILA. Oh, Lady Etherington – the cheque for this evening. Oh, bother! Now, where's that husband of mine? Dennis? Where are you?

DENNIS. I'm right here, Sheila.

SHEILA. I can see that. Now have you seen the programmes? The least we can do this evening is hand out the programmes.

DENNIS. The programmes are still being printed. We've had the devil's own job finding out details about everyone.

SHEILA. Never mind about that now. We have more important matters to consider.

DENNIS. Perhaps we could ask the audience to leave. Just until we get ourselves organised.

SHEILA. I don't think so, Dennis.

DENNIS. Why not?

SHEILA. I don't suppose they'll come back.

DENNIS. A bit like our cast then.

SHEILA. What's that supposed to mean?

DENNIS. You did give them a hard time during rehearsal this afternoon.

SHEILA. No more than they deserved.

DENNIS. You treat people like children.

SHEILA. That's not true!

DENNIS. You have to understand that people join our group because they want to enjoy themselves – not be bullied.

SHEILA. How dare you! I'm not a bully!

DENNIS. Look how you treat Louise and Carol.

SHEILA. Louise is as thick as two short planks and Carol deserves all she gets.

DENNIS. I don't think anyone deserves the lash end of your tongue.

SHEILA. Let's just get on, shall we? We have an audience out there. Now, where is everyone? I particularly want to speak to Carol again.   **DENNIS EXITS**

ENTER CAROL

CAROL. *(To the audience)* I think there's going to be trouble tonight. As you can see, it's all a bit of a cock-up. Not surprising really, given the organisational skills around here. And as for Sheila, I don't think Her Majesty approves of me.

SHEILA. Carol, do you mind? You're determined to ruin this evening, aren't you?

CAROL. It doesn't look like it needs me to ruin it.

SHEILA. If you can't say, or do, anything helpful, then don't say, or do, anything at all.

CAROL. I've already put forward a reasonable suggestion.

SHEILA. And what would that be?

CAROL. Let's do what we can. Even if we just go through a few scenes, it'll be something.

SHEILA. You really have no idea, do you?

CAROL. I can recognise a disaster when I see one.

SHEILA. *(Fuming)* Just leave it, Carol! Okay?

CAROL. Right! Have it your own way! See if I care! Sort it out yourself! I'm going to get my coat!

SHEILA. What on earth for?

CAROL. I've had enough of this. I'm off! You can find yourself another actress.

SHEILA. I didn't know we had one in the first place.

CAROL. We've got plenty of Prima Donnas, if that's what you mean?

SHEILA. Sometimes, Carol –

CAROL. What? Threats now, is it?

SHEILA. I have no need to threaten you.

CAROL. It's about time someone put you in your place.

SHEILA. No need! I'm going for a bit of fresh air! You stay here! You can talk to Louise – you're both dizzy enough for each other.

SHEILA EXITS

ENTER LOUISE

LOUISE. What's wrong with Sheila?

CAROL. What's right with her?

LOUISE. I can't do anything right today.

CAROL. Don't get upset. It's not your fault this evening's such a mess.

LOUISE. It's not that.

CAROL. Then what?

LOUISE. It's Malcolm. It's no more than I can expect, I suppose.

CAROL. I don't understand.

LOUISE. Who's going to look at frumpy old me when I have to act next to somebody like you?

CAROL. You're not frumpy.

LOUISE. Yes, I am.

CAROL. Now Sheila – she's frumpy.

LOUISE. *(Smiling)* You can't say that!

CAROL. You look nice when you smile.

LOUISE. Do I?

CAROL. What's Malcolm done exactly?

LOUISE. Nothing, really. It's just – he's been ignoring me. And when we do go out together, all he does is sit looking miserable. He does talk about you, though. Says what a wonderful actress you are.

CAROL. Hardly. I've not been in the group that long.

LOUISE. He says you're a natural. I try to ignore it, but he just carries on.

CAROL. I'm glad somebody thinks so.

CAROL EXITS

ENTER SHEILA

SHEILA. *(Overhearing Louise)* Perhaps if you weren't so obliging, Louise.

LOUISE. What's that supposed to mean?

SHEILA. Confront him. After all, you and Malcolm are supposed to be engaged.

LOUISE. It's more an understanding really.

SHEILA. Sounds like a misunderstanding to me.

LOUISE. Can we make a start, please?

SHEILA. *(Suddenly defeated)* Oh, I don't know. It's all so hopeless.

LOUISE. Maybe some of the others will turn up.

SHEILA. I don't think so. We barely had enough at this afternoon's rehearsal.

LOUISE. Numbers do seem to be dropping.

SHEILA. People just don't seem to be able to commit themselves these days.

LOUISE. It's the sign of the times.

SHEILA. When I first joined this group, we had at least twenty people for each show. But since I became Artistic Director –

LOUISE. People come and go.

SHEILA. And since that Carol joined the group -

LOUISE. I don't know what we're doing here anyway.

SHEILA. We were asked to put on a show.

LOUISE. But in a community hall?

SHEILA. These bookings are very lucrative. Community halls pay a fortune for people like us to come in and perform.

LOUISE. I can't think why.

SHEILA. *(Looking around)* Never mind all that, I haven't seen Malcolm all evening. Where on earth is he? Louise, will you go and find him?

LOUISE EXITS

ENTER MALCOLM

SHEILA. Malcolm, where on earth have you been?

MALCOLM. I've been phoning the police.

SHEILA. I know your performance this afternoon wasn't brilliant, but it's hardly a hanging offence.

MALCOLM. Someone's been murdered.

SHEILA. What? Who?

MALCOLM. The woman who booked us this evening. Lady Etherington-Smythe. She's been stabbed.

SHEILA. Where?

MALCOLM. In her car.

SHEILA. I mean, where on her person?

MALCOLM. I don't know. In the chest, I think.

SHEILA. Oh, this is dreadful.

MALCOLM. She ain't too pleased either.

SHEILA. Who found her?

MALCOLM. I did. I was in the car park, having a fag. I heard a noise. Didn't think much of it at first. But I then got curious. Went over to this posh car, looked inside and there she was. Dead as a dodo.

SHEILA. How awful.

MALCOLM. Talking of which, at least we don't have to bother with a performance this evening.

SHEILA. What are we going to do while we wait for the police to arrive?

MALCOLM. Dunno about you, but I'm going outside for another fag.

THEY EXIT

FADE

TWO

ENTER INSPECTOR MICHAELS AND SHEILA

SHEILA. I'm sorry, Inspector. There's nothing more I can add.

MICHAELS. You say Lady Etherington-Smythe booked you to perform this play of yours.

SHEILA. Months ago. It was a coincidence really. We were at school together. Different years.

MICHAELS. You do move in exalted circles.

SHEILA. Not really. She was plain Daisy Smith then. As you can see, she's done well for herself. Or rather did well for herself, until this evening.

MICHAELS. I understand her husband's the chairman of this community hall.

SHEILA. He swans around the place, if that's what you mean. Maybe he killed his wife -

MICHAELS. Lord Etherington-Smythe seems to have a watertight alibi.

SHEILA. I can't think why anyone would want to kill Daisy Smith.

MICHAELS. Something from her past perhaps?

SHEILA. I couldn't possibly say.

MICHAELS. You say your company were late in arriving here this evening?

SHEILA. Half the company still haven't turned up.

MICHAELS. What were you planning on doing?

SHEILA. We were going to do a few scenes from our play. God knows what though.

MICHAELS. I suppose I'd better interview some of the others.

SHEILA. The first one you want to speak to is Carol. She's the newest member of the group.

MICHAELS. Then I shall speak to Carol. Can you fetch her. **SHEILA EXITS**

ENTER CAROL

CAROL. I don't care what Sheila says about me. I joined the group because she asked me to join. It was the autumn fete. She couldn't get me into her clutches fast enough.

MICHAELS. It doesn't sound like you and your artistic director get on too well.

CAROL. I don't understand her. She's bright and intelligent. What's this need to control the group?

MICHAELS. Tell me, did you know Lady Etherington-Smythe?

CAROL. I know she booked us for this evening. But Louise handled the booking.

MICHAELS. I understand there was a problem with the booking.

CAROL. Sheila most probably gave Louise the wrong time in the first place.

MICHAELS. So, let me get this right. You were all supposed to be here at – what time?

CAROL. Seven. Louise got it down as being eight.

MICHAELS. So, the moment of Lady Etherington-Smythe's death would have coincided with the whole company being present and correct.

CAROL. We'd have been half-way through the performance.

MICHAELS. Therefore it would be safe to assume that Lady Etherington-Smythe's body wouldn't have been discovered until after the show.

CAROL. I guess not. Unless the audience decided to walk out on us in disgust. It wouldn't have been the first time.

MICHAELS. Tell me, what was the title of tonight's little performance?

CAROL. *Death of a Theatre Director*.

MICHAELS. Mmmm! You can go now. I would like to speak to this Louise woman.

CAROL EXITS

ENTER LOUISE

MICHAELS. Ah, you must be Louise.

LOUISE. What a tragedy.

MICHAEL. What, you being called Louise?

LOUISE. It's my own fault, I suppose.

MICHAELS. I beg your pardon?

LOUISE. If I behave like a doormat – I can't really be surprised when everyone decides to wipe their feet on me.

MICHAELS. I don't understand.

LOUISE. *(Upset)* People simply can't treat me like this!

MICHAELS. Like what?

LOUISE. You know what I mean.

MICHAELS. I don't know what you mean – that's the whole point.

LOUISE. I suppose Malcolm would rather be with Carol. I just don't want to get hurt.

MICHAELS. Nobody's going to hurt you.

LOUISE. I just don't like to be treated like a fool.

MICHAELS. Nobody's treating you like a fool.

LOUISE. You should speak to Malcolm. I must go and find the booking form. I'm sure I got the time right.

MICHAELS. Where is this Malcolm?

LOUISE. He's most probably outside having a cigarette. I'll go and fetch him.

LOUISE EXITS

ENTER MALCOLM

MALCOLM. Did someone mention my name?

MICHAELS. Tell me, Malcolm, how long have you and Louise been seeing each other?

MALCOLM. About four years.

MICHAELS. How did you meet?

MALCOLM. She was in the pub with her mates.

MICHAELS. Love at first sight?

MALCOLM. Not really. We got talking. We then went to the pictures. It sort of drifted on from there.

MICHAELS. How long have you been doing this acting lark?

MALCOLM. Longer than I care to remember. Louise roped me into it a couple of years ago. I've been around ever since.

MICHAELS. What do you do for a living?

MALCOLM. I'm a buyer. For an engineering firm.

MICHAELS. Do you enjoy it?

MALCOLM. It's okay. It's a means of making money, nothing more.

MICHAELS. No ambitions?

MALCOLM. I quite fancy going into management. But we'll see.

MICHAELS. So, here you are, the mainstay of the group.

MALCOLM. Hardly. The group's in terminal decay, I'm afraid. That's why there's so much bitching going on. People have nothing better to do.

MICHAELS. Young Carol seems to have triggered off her fair share of bitching.

MALCOLM. She's a natural talent. People don't like that in an actress.

MICHAELS. Tell me, did you know Lady Etherington-Smythe.

MALCOLM. Of course I knew her. Her husband owns the engineering company I work for. Now, if you'll excuse me.

MALCOLM EXITS

ENTER SHEILA

SHEILA. *(On her mobile)* That's it! I've had enough. The rest of the cast are at home watching *EastEnders*. Why the hell they can't video it like the rest of us is beyond me.

MICHAELS. Problems?

SHEILA. We might as well all go home.

MICHAELS. Sorry. Not possible.

SHEILA. Why not?

MICHAELS. There's been a murder here, that's why not.

SHEILA. Surely that's got nothing to do with us.

MICHAELS. You and Carol. You don't appear to get on all that well.

SHEILA. We have values in this group. And I refuse to see those values undermined by someone like – like -

MICHAELS. Carol?

SHEILA. I refuse to lower myself. I don't know why she doesn't just leave the group. Carol's a bitch! An absolute bitch!

MICHAELS. I appear to have arrived on the scene just in time.

SHEILA. Hardly, Lady Etherington-Smythe is dead, you know.

MICHAELS. I meant in order to prevent another murder taking place.

SHEILA. Who?

MICHAELS. Young Carol – with yourself being chief suspect.

SHEILA. You're barking up the wrong tree, Inspector.

MICHAELS. The only person I haven't seen this evening is your husband, Dennis.

SHEILA. He's never around when you want him.

MICHAELS. I have a sergeant exactly the same.

SHEILA. I'll see if I can rustle Dennis up for you.

SHEILA EXITS

ENTER DENNIS

DENNIS. I really must apologise for my wife, Inspector. She gets a bit – you know.

MICHAELS. But she hasn't done anything wrong.

DENNIS. Then what –

MICHAELS. She and Carol -

DENNIS. Carol refuses to be browbeaten into submission. She joined this group to act and act she will. My wife has no right to wage a campaign against her. She thinks Carol's some sort of tart, you know.

MICHAELS. And is she?

DENNIS. Hardly –

MICHAELS. Come on, Dennis. You clearly have no idea how women behave – especially women who feel under threat – imaginary or otherwise.

DENNIS. I'm sure that's not true.

MICHAELS. I understand Carol's a divorcee.

DENNIS. I really don't see –

MICHAELS. Your wife most probably disapproves of Carol.

DENNIS. My wife rarely goes by first impressions alone. She likes to think about a person before making her mind up. She certainly wouldn't hold Carol's divorce against her.

MICHAELS. Do you know why Carol's marriage ended?

DENNIS. I imagine that to be a private matter –

MICHAELS. In cases of murder, there are no private matters.

DENNIS. Then I suggest you speak to Carol.

MICHAELS. I intend to. But first, I must speak to your dear wife again.

ENTER SHEILA

SHEILA. Dennis, what are you doing?

DENNIS. I'm chatting to the Inspector here.

SHEILA. I can see that! Perhaps you could do something useful for a change.

DENNIS. There isn't much to do, is there?

SHEILA. You don't do much at the best of times.

DENNIS. I do as much as any hen-pecked husband does.

SHEILA. You're not hen-pecked.

DENNIS. Who says?

SHEILA. I say!

DENNIS. Precisely!

SHEILA. What's that supposed to mean?

MICHAELS. May I make a suggestion?

SHEILA/DENNIS. No!

DENNIS. Why do you always have to feel so persecuted, Sheila?

SHEILA. Persecuted? Me?

DENNIS. Yes. And you always have to sneer at things.

SHEILA. I don't sneer!

DENNIS. God! You can be bloody impossible at times.

SHEILA. I've been through a great deal this evening.

DENNIS. There's still no need to lose your sense of humour – if you ever had one -

SHEILA. I have a sense of humour – when I find something worth laughing at. But when I find my authority being undermined –

DENNIS. There's nobody undermining your authority. You're being paranoid. It's about time you loosened up a little.

SHEILA. Loosened up! How dare you!

DENNIS. I dare all right! I'm not having you behave like a spoilt brat!

MICHAELS. *(Interrupting)* All right, you two! Enough is enough. We <u>do</u> have a murder enquiry on our hands. Now, let us look at the facts. Lady Etherington-Smythe booked your company to put on a play this evening.

SHEILA. Correct.

MICHAELS. She booked you for seven o'clock but for some unforeseen reason, you all arrived an hour late.

SHEILA. That stupid woman Louise got the booking wrong.

MICHAELS. No sooner had you arrived, Lady Etherington-Smythe departed only to meet her maker in the car park.

SHEILA. Who on earth would have a motive for killing her?

MICHAELS. You say you knew her at school.

SHEILA. So? Hardly a motive for murder!

MICHAELS. Did you know Carol was having an affair with Lady Etherington-Smythe's husband?

SHEILA. How on earth did you know that, Inspector?

MICHAELS. I've been chatting to the domiciliary facilities manager of this hall. Very informative he is too. Although gossip is rather hard to prove. Which leaves Louise and Malcolm.

SHEILA. You can count Louise out. She's too dozy to kill anyone. And as for Malcolm, he has no possible motive for any of this.

ENTER MALCOLM. HE HAS BEEN STABBED

SHEILA. Oh my God! It's Malcolm. He's been stabbed! Let's get him off before he spills too much blood on the carpet.

THEY EXIT WITH MALCOLM. FADE

THREE

ENTER MICHAELS AND LOUISE

MICHAELS. I'm afraid I have to ask you a few questions, Louise.

LOUISE. It simply wasn't going to work.

MICHAELS. What wasn't going to work?

LOUISE. Men. They're all the same. Self, self, self.

MICHAELS. I don't understand.

LOUISE. Malcolm obviously wasn't ready for a relationship.

MICHAELS. He certainly isn't now.

LOUISE. We would see each other once or twice a week at rehearsals. Apart from that, we did what? Go to the pub?

MICHAELS. Then why didn't you do something different? You could have gone to the cinema. Or perhaps a night club.

LOUISE. It's finished. Malcolm and I.

MICHAELS. You can say that again.

LOUISE. I just need to tell him.

MICHAELS. I think he's got the picture.

LOUISE. What do you mean?

MICHAELS. Well, he's dead, of course.

LOUISE. Who's dead?

MICHAELS. Malcolm.

LOUISE. Why did nobody tell me? This can't be happening.

SHE EXITS IN TEARS

ENTER SHEILA

SHEILA. First Lady Etherington-Smythe and now Malcolm. I don't know what to say anymore. There used to be a sense of order in this group. A sense of belonging. Values. A certain integrity. Then Carol came along.

MICHAELS. I would have thought a woman like Carol would have better things to do on an evening.

SHEILA. Someone like Carol breezes in here – it must be nice to have life so easy.

MICHAELS. We all have burdens to carry.

SHEILA. I don't feel I belong in this group anymore.

MICHAELS. Of course you do. You're all part of the same team.

SHEILA. It used to be my team.

MICHAELS. You used to belong to it. There's a difference.

SHEILA. Too much has happened. The rows. The surprises. The upsets.

MICHAELS. I really don't think Louise had anything to do with Malcolm's death.

SHEILA. But Louise and Malcolm were always bickering. And she was in an out in the car park for most of the evening. She kept on looking for her blessed booking form. She was convinced she got the time right. And as for Malcolm, he smokes like a chimney. That always takes him out in the car park.

MICHAELS. Perhaps he saw something relating to Lady Etherington-Smythe's death and that led to his own demise.

SHEILA. They do say smoking can damage your health.

MICHAELS. I think it's time I spoke to some of the others. Your husband, Dennis, for a start.

SHEILA. I'll go and fetch him.

MICHAELS. No, you stay here. I'll go and find him. It's about time I wound this case up. I also need to speak to Louise. I have an idea.

MICHAELS EXITS

ENTER DENNIS

DENNIS. Look, Sheila. I'm sorry about what happened. Maybe we can go for an Italian meal tomorrow night? To make up for a lousy evening. That would be nice.

SHEILA. Dennis?

DENNIS. What?

SHEILA. I hate to have to say this.

DENNIS. Say what?

SHEILA. We go to the Italian every week.

DENNIS. It's our little treat. Time away from this lot.

SHEILA. I know, but –

DENNIS. But what?

SHEILA. I don't actually like Italian.

DENNIS. I beg your pardon?

SHEILA. Well, I do. But to tell you the truth – to be perfectly honest – I'd rather go somewhere else – for a change. The theatre perhaps. I think *The Mousetrap* is still running.

DENNIS. You never said.

SHEILA. Are you upset?

DENNIS. Of course I'm not upset.

ENTER MICHAELS

MICHAELS. *(Clearing his throat)* I'm sorry to have to break up this cosy reconciliation, but we do have two murders to deal with.

DENNIS. I'm sorry I can't help, Inspector.

MICHAELS. What was Malcolm doing outside in the car park?

DENNIS. He was having a fag. He's not been getting on well with Louise, he just wanted the space.

MICHAELS. He's certainly going to get his fair share of space now – six foot of it.

DENNIS. He's also been having trouble at work. Ask Carol, she knows more about it than me.

MICHAELS. I think I shall. Where is Carol?

DENNIS. I'll go and fetch her.

SHEILA. Not on your own you won't!

THEY BOTH EXIT AS CAROL ENTERS

CAROL. I suppose it's bound to come out, sooner or later. Malcolm was having an affair with Lady Etherington-Smythe.

MICHAELS. She's not his type, surely.

CAROL. She wasn't born with a plum in her mouth. Daisy Smith, her name was. Common as muck. You ask Sheila. They were at school together.

MICHAELS. How did you know that?

CAROL. I was at the same school. We just didn't know each other. Different years, different circle of friends. It only really came out when Louise started doing the programme for the show. She asked me to help compile biographies. There wasn't much to say about anyone so we had to delve into peoples' personal histories.

MICHAELS. So everyone was connected to everyone else.

CAROL. More or less!

MICHAELS. So what was your connection to Lord Etherington-Smythe?

CAROL. I'm recently divorced, Inspector. Some men find that attractive in a woman. They see a divorced woman as a challenge – they think they're gagging for it!

MICHAELS. I daresay it makes you somewhat notorious.

CAROL. I liked to get about, Inspector. Try new things – aerobics, running, swimming.

MICHAELS. What about sex?

CAROL. Inspector! I know these are liberal times, but I hardly know you!

MICHAELS. Let me guess. Coming here was supposed to be a new beginning for you. Joining this group was going to give you chance to start afresh. Then you met Lord Etherington-Smythe.

CAROL. That's amazing!

MICHAELS. All in a day's work.

CAROL. But I didn't kill Lady Etherington-Smythe, Inspector. I'm not a murderer.

MICHAELS. One of you is, and I intend to find out who. Let's see if Dennis and Sheila know anything more. Where are they?

THEY EXIT AS DENNIS AND SHEILA ENTER

DENNIS. I'm sorry, Sheila. I've just been talking to Louise.

SHEILA. So?

DENNIS. She says you killed Lady Etherington-Smythe.

SHEILA. I beg your pardon?

DENNIS. She saw you and Lady Etherington-Smythe arguing in the car park.

SHEILA. We weren't arguing. I just wanted paying for this evening.

DENNIS. That's not what Louise told me. She told me you were trying to blackmail Lady Etherington-Smythe. You were going to tell the world about her affair with Malcolm. She was going to report you to the police. You pulled a knife -

SHEILA. Dennis, how could you believe such lies?

DENNIS. And the Inspector is right. You altered Louise's forms on purpose. You wanted as much time as possible to elapse between the start of our show and the discovery of Lady Etherington-Smythe's body.

SHEILA. The length of the show is the same, whether it starts at seven or eight.

DENNIS. Ah, but if we started late, the audience would be in such a hurry to go home that they'd miss the parked car with a murdered body in the driving seat.

SHEILA. I didn't kill Lady Etherington-Smythe. Will nobody believe me?

ENTER CAROL AND MICHAELS

CAROL. I believe you, Sheila.

MICHAELS. It's about time somebody shed some light on this story.

CAROL. Sheila didn't kill Lady Etherington-Smythe. Louise did. And she's trying to shift the blame.

MICHAELS. I think you'd better explain.

CAROL. Lady Etherington-Smythe was a bit of a slapper. She enjoyed a bit of rough and you don't get much rougher than our friend Malcolm. Malcolm and Lady Etherington-Smythe were having an affair. Malcolm met her at a works do. Don't forget, Malcolm worked for Lord Etherington-Smythe's engineering company.

MICHAELS. How come you know so much?

CAROL. I was outside in the car park. I'd just had one of my regular rows with Sheila and I wanted some fresh air. Malcolm followed me and started to try it on. The man just wouldn't take no for an answer. We struggled. Then Louise turned up. She went spare. She accused Malcolm of all sorts.

MICHAELS. So, what happened then?

CAROL. Louise had a knife in her hand. It was covered in blood. Malcolm tried to take the knife off her.

MICHAELS. Why didn't you try and stop them?

CAROL. Are you kidding? I'm not taking on a demented woman waving a knife.

MICHAELS. What happened then?

CAROL. I'm not sure exactly. Both went off into the night. The next thing I knew was when Malcolm came staggering through here. He must have taken ages to snuff it. I suspect it's the only thing he did take his time over.

MICHAELS. *(Looking around)* Where is Louise, by the way?

ENTER LOUISE, STABBED. SHE IS CLUTCHING A PIECE OF PAPER

MICHAELS. Oh my God! It's another death.

SHEILA. It's Louise. Stabbed!

MICHAELS. Quick! We must get her off.

THEY DRAG LOUSE OFF

FADE

FOUR

ENTER MICHAELS AND SHEILA

SHEILA. *(With a blood-stained piece of paper)* I'm sorry, Inspector. I can't work out the handwriting. The form is all covered in blood.

MICHAELS. But you will agree that the time has been changed.

SHEILA. It would appear that Louise was right about the time of this evening's performance. Someone has altered the seven o'clock start to eight o'clock. But why would someone do that?

MICHAELS. To delay proceedings. To cover their tracks. That person wanted to confuse matters by having the cast arrive late. If you started your show at eight and not seven, Lady Etherington-Smythe's body wouldn't be discovered until gone eleven. Putting as much time between the murder and discovery as possible.

SHEILA. A bit feeble, don't you think?

MICHAELS. Then things started to go wrong. Half your actors failed to turn up at all. You didn't start at eight. Your company is in a bit of a mess. With all the bickering, it was inevitable that some of the actors would go outside for a fag and a bit of fresh air. One of those people was Malcolm who most probably saw the murder take place.

SHEILA. Why didn't Malcolm report the murderer to the police?

MICHAELS. He saw who the murderer was and decided to blackmail him – or her. He wasn't fussy where his money came from and he wanted to get away from Louise and start afresh.

SHEILA. And what about Louise? Why on earth was she killed?

MICHAELS. She had the only real evidence there was – the altered booking form. The murderer had to get hold of the form in order to cover his – or her – tracks.

SHEILA. So who is the killer?

MICHAELS. I think we can look forward to one more twist in the tale.

ENTER A RECOVERED BUT BLOOD-STAINED LOUISE

SHEILA. Louise!

LOUISE. I am determined to get one thing right this evening.

SHEILA. But you're dead.

LOUISE. A trick of the trade. It didn't take much to raid the props cupboard and get a retractable knife.

SHEILA. But why the hoax?

LOUISE. To help unearth the real murderer.

SHEILA. I think you'd better explain.

LOUISE. Oh, I'll explain. Malcolm was having an affair with Lady Etherington-Smythe all right. I've known about it for some time.

SHEILA. I hope you've paid for using our props.

LOUISE. But Lady Etherington-Smythe wasn't the only one receiving Malcolm's attentions. He's been sniffing around Carol from the first day she turned up. But unlike me, Carol's not the gentle type. She knew about Malcolm and Lady Etherington-Smythe and decided to kill two lying toads with one stab of a knife! Don't forget, Carol was also having an affair with Lord Etherington-Smythe.

SHEILA. How do you know all this?

LOUISE. I went out to the car park to find my booking form. I saw Malcolm sneaking over towards Lady Etherington-Smythe's car.

MICHAELS. Then what happened?

LOUISE. Sheila turned up and had a row with Lady Etherington-Smythe – I couldn't hear about what. Then Sheila walked away and Malcolm joined Lady Etherington-Smythe. They started to kiss and hug and other things – I was so upset. But I was also paralysed with fear. Then Malcolm left. Then Carol turned up. I couldn't believe my eyes. She simply got into the car next to Lady Etherington-Smythe, there was a quick scuffle and Carol got out and walked away.

SHEILA. So when was Malcolm killed?

LOUISE. Later on. I was still looking for my booking form. I saw Malcolm and Carol arguing in the car park. Carol was beside herself. She just stabbed him, there and then. She saw me and I ran away.

MICHAELS. That's when Louise came to me. We decided to fake her death so as to afford Carol an alibi. It's always best to allow a murderer enough rope – eventually they'll hang themselves.

ENTER THE SERGEANT

MICHAELS. *(To the Sergeant)* Sergeant, find Miss Carol and arrest her. I think this enquiry has come to an end.

THE SERGEANT EXITS

SHEILA. Tell me, Inspector. Do you come across many murders in your job?

MICHAELS. A few.

SHEILA. Except this evening we've had a hat-trick of killings.

MICHAELS. No we haven't. We've just had two murders and a fake.

SHEILA. Something's just occurred to me, Inspector. Your nice Sergeant does know Carol has a knife and isn't afraid to use it. I wouldn't want her causing any further injury with it.

ENTER THE SERGEANT, STABBED

MICHAELS. Whoops! That makes our hat trick for the evening.

FADE

END OF PLAY

FOREST MURDER MYSTERY

By

John Dunne

<u>Characters</u>
Innkeeper
Gypsy
Mistress Quigley
Young Alice
Quack Doctor
Young Jack
Smuggler Nick
The Reverend

Set in a dark, mysterious forest amid witchcraft,
smuggling and of course murder – the play paints a dark
picture of a bygone age.

ONE

ENTER THE INNKEEPER AND GYPSY

INNKEEPER. *(Carrying a bottle)* Come on! Let's be having you.

GYPSY. Get lost! You're drunk! Again!

INNKEEPER. You what?

GYPSY. If you want to run this inn, then run it. Just leave me out of it.

INNKEEPER. You do as I tell you!

GYPSY. I don't like this inn. And as for the forest hereabouts – it's an evil place.

INNKEEPER. Rubbish! This forest is no different from any other place in the land.

GYPSY. It's true what I say. Folk here have no smiles on their faces and will stab you between the shoulders for the price of a drink.

INNKEEPER. You're just an idle old sow, too lazy to move yourself.

GYPSY. The men go on the drink for days on end.

INNKEEPER. I'm glad to hear it. It'll be good for business.

GYPSY. Young girls and woodland creatures be not safe.

INNKEEPER. Since you are neither a young girl or a woodland creature –

GYPSY. The women here smoke clay pipes and have their babies out in the wilds.

INNKEEPER. Why should that concern us?

GYPSY. They intermarry with their cousins and raise stubborn offspring who be strong in arm and thick in the head.

INNKEEPER. I care not what they do, as long as they patronise my inn and pay for your company when they become more amorous.

GYPSY. All they get from life is what they can poach or smuggle. Such people know not the meaning of money. They live by barter and haggle. Ask them the time of day and they'll charge you a pig for it.

INNKEEPER. Painting a black picture cannot change things.

GYPSY. This be no place for folk like us. We be not welcome here.

INNKEEPER. We be as welcome here as any other place.

GYPSY. They think we carry the pox. They think the inn is a den of vice.

INNKEEPER. It wouldn't be so bad if you were half ways a beauty – but you be nothing of the sort. Why I should harness my fate to a whittering gypsy woman, God alone knows.

GYPSY. If you don't like my whitter, my race or my sex, then harness your fate elsewhere.

INNKEEPER. Don't push what little luck you have, my dear. I might just do that.

GYPSY. Then you would have to find someone else mad enough to slave for you.

INNKEEPER. Enough of this bickering, we have an inn to run.

GYPSY. You're nothing but an ignorant swine! You take far too much upon yourself. It's time I took myself a new man.

INNKEEPER. Sometimes you strain my temper, woman. So, come along now, we have guests to attend to.

GYPSY. What guests? Do you call the people who frequent this inn guests? They are nothing but vagabonds and thieves. I'm surprised this place hasn't been closed down.

INNKEEPER. The Magistrate and I have an understanding.

GYPSY. You mean you have him in your pocket.

INNKEEPER. He does well enough out of my activities.

GYPSY. You're not the only one who has an understanding with the Magistrate.

INNKEEPER. Oh, yes. Do you offer him a discount for spoilt goods, or what?

GYPSY. Never you mind what I offer the Magistrate. *(She takes out a pistol)*

INNKEEPER. What are you doing with that pistol?

GYPSY. Like I said, we live in dangerous times.

THE GYPSY EXITS

ENTER MISTRESS QUIGLEY

INNKEEPER. And what do you want?

QUIGLEY. I only want a bite to eat.

INNKEEPER. If I've told you once -

QUIGLEY. You'll want me soon enough when you fall ill with the plague.

INNKEEPER. There's no plague around these parts.

QUIGLEY. Don't you believe it.

INNKEEPER. And besides, if I want doctoring, I'll call for a real doctor.

QUIGLEY. There are others who appreciate my arts.

INNKEEPER. Then go to them for shelter. I'm running an inn here, not a doss house. *(He looks at her)* Some say you're a witch, you know.

QUIGLEY. Some say many things.

INNKEEPER. But I don't believe a word of it.

QUIGLEY. Maybe you should.

INNKEEPER. Maybe I should turf you out on the street.

QUIGLEY. I don't know why I want to stay here anyway. This place has surely seen better days.

INNKEEPER. This is the best inn for miles. Mind you, the only thing we haven't got is a haunting. Old inns like this are often haunted. Maybe I should cultivate the odd ghost. Hauntings can do wonders for trade. People can be very morbid about such matters.

QUIGLEY. So what about a bite to eat then?

INNKEEPER. Clear off, you old hag!

QUIGLEY. A curse upon you.

INNKEEPER. Curse away.

QUIGLEY EXITS

ENTER ALICE

ALICE. Who was that?

INNKEEPER. Oh, Mistress Quigley, making a pest of herself again.

ALICE. You should be careful. They say she can cast spells.

INNKEEPER. If she could cast spells she wouldn't be scrounging around here for a scrap to eat.

ALICE. Just be careful, that's all.

INNKEEPER. Enough of her. Are we due a delivery tonight?

ALICE. All being well.

INNKEEPER. Good. And what of your father?

ALICE. What of him?

INNKEEPER. I think he suspects.

ALICE. He knows nothing of my involvement.

INNKEEPER. Then we must keep it that way.

ALICE. (*Looking around the place*) I wish I could work here all the time.

INNKEEPER. You will, soon. Once you stand up to your father –

ALICE. Father is under a lot of strain. I don't want to be a burden to him.

INNKEEPER. I'm sure you're nothing of the sort.

ALICE. I must go. Father is entertaining the Magistrate tonight. Both insist I be there. The Magistrate is a strange man, he always looks at me with interest.

INNKEEPER. As do many men, my dear. It is something you must get used to.

ALICE. I know well the looks of men. But the Magistrate looks on me – almost as a daughter.

INNKEEPER. Never mind all that. It is important you keep both men occupied – tonight of all nights.

ALICE EXITS

ENTER A QUACK DOCTOR

DOCTOR. *(Carrying a bag)* Excuse me, I'm looking for somewhere to stay.

INNKEEPER. Then you have come to the right place, sir.

DOCTOR. I am a doctor, from London.

INNKEEPER. So what brings you here, doctor?

DOCTOR. Business. I'll be staying here for a couple of days, if that's all right with you?

INNKEEPER. It's all the same to me, sir. Perhaps you would like to freshen up before dinner?

DOCTOR. Before I do that, do you know the local doctor around here?

INNKEEPER. We don't have a regular doctor.

DOCTOR. Oh, I see. Perhaps I could fulfil a valuable role here in the village.

INNKEEPER. Shall I take your bag, sir?

THE INNKEEPER REACHES FOR THE DOCTOR'S BAG. THE DOCTOR SNATCHES IT AWAY

DOCTOR. No! That's perfectly all right.

INNKEEPER. Then come this way, doctor.

THE DOCTOR EXITS

ENTER JACK

JACK. Who is that?

INNKEEPER. A doctor, from London.

JACK. He looks shifty. Maybe he's carrying valuables on his person.

INNKEEPER. He certainly kept that bag close to his chest.

JACK. If only we could get our hands on it.

INNKEEPER. Perhaps we can.

JACK. You're not saying we should rob him?

INNKEEPER. Why not?

JACK. Robbing him will be easier said than done.

INNKEEPER. Then we'll just have to dispose of the body.

JACK. You don't mean kill him?

INNKEEPER. I wasn't proposing to wrap him up in cotton wool and return him to his mother.

JACK. How on earth will you kill him?

INNKEEPER. I won't. You will. When he's asleep, you creep into his room and bash him over the head.

JACK. And what will you be doing while all this bashing is going on?

INNKEEPER. I'll be keeping watch.

JACK. And how will we get rid of the body?

INNKEEPER. We fill his pockets with rocks and drop him down the disused well at the back of the inn.

JACK. I see, I take all the risk and you take all the profit. Charming!

INNKEEPER. It'll be like taking sweetmeats from a baby.

JACK EXITS

ENTER NICK

NICK. The barrels will be arriving tonight.

INNKEEPER. Just make sure you're quiet about it. You're supposed to be smugglers, not town criers.

NICK. We'll have to get the horses from the Reverend's stable. That'll make our lives easier.

INNKEEPER. Do what you will. Just don't make a song and dance about it.

NICK. I must say, the Reverend wasn't too pleased the last time we borrowed his horses.

INNKEEPER. I wouldn't worry about the Reverend. He's dining with the Magistrate tonight.

NICK. A bit risky, isn't it?

INNKEEPER. Alice is there to look out for us.

NICK. It's a pity the girl can't use her charms on the Magistrate. I hear he is partial to young female company. It would make our lives much easier.

INNKEEPER. Alice is to have nothing to do with tonight's adventure, or any other escapade! Do I make myself clear?

NICK. I'm only saying.

INNKEEPER. Well don't! You're job is to do what you're told.

NICK. The Reverend wouldn't be so righteous if he knew his daughter was involved. And she is a comely creature.

INNKEEPER. How dare you talk like that! You men know not how to conduct yourselves at times.

NICK. Sorry Boss.

INNKEEPER. And stop hanging around. You're bound to attract attention to yourself.

NICK EXITS

ENTER THE GYPSY

GYPSY. This is a dark country.

INNKEEPER. What is it now?

GYPSY. There is danger. There be forces of which we be ignorant. Can you not feel it?

INNKEEPER. I can feel something - irritation at your prattle.

GYPSY. Can't you feel the evil? Watching us?

INNKEEPER. Look, let's get one thing straight. You may wish to peddle your wares under the guise of being a noble gypsy, but don't try to fool me with your masquerade.

GYPSY. It's no masquerade. I come from a long and noble line of Romany travellers.

INNKEEPER. You're nothing but a clapped-out tinker with an ever-active imagination and a vivid choice in clothing.

GYPSY. How dare you say that!

INNKEEPER. As it happens, it suits me to have an exotic companion working for me. The lads are quite happy to spend money on a woman of mature years as long as they imagine they're paying for something unusual.

GYPSY. I don't have to put up with these insults. I have the art. I can see matters which are invisible to the heathen eye. I can peer into the future and foretell events. I can delve into the souls of men and women and pluck out their destinies.

INNKEEPER. If you're so good at all that, why can't you make a better living?

GYPSY. It's circumstances which make people do things against their wishes. And you cannot fool me. I can see into your heart easy enough. You dislike your lot in the world as much as I do. Why else do you seek solace in a bottle?

INNKEEPER. I seek solace in a bottle because it helps deaden my head to the drone of your voice.

GYPSY. You used to have so many dreams.

INNKEEPER. Enough of this drivel. You have work to do. We have a new guest. A doctor. I want you to entertain him. I believe him to be carrying valuables on his person.

THE GYPSY EXITS

ENTER NICK

A STORM IS BREWING

NICK. This storm's going to be a godsend to us.

INNKEEPER. Aye, it's going to be dark, and no moon about.

NICK. It will take a keen Excise Man indeed to venture out on a night like this.

THERE IS A CRY

NICK. Listen! I thought I heard a cry.

INNKEEPER. It's only the wind clapping through the trees.

NICK. They say the trees contain the souls of dead men. And when the wind is up, the poor creatures cry out in agony.

INNKEEPER. They do say a great deal, and you do listen a great deal. Perhaps you should shack up with the gypsy woman.

THERE IS A PISTOL SHOT, FOLLOWED BY ANOTHER

NICK. Quick! It's the Revenue! We must away!

INNKEEPER. We must return to our hearth. There's to be blood spilt tonight.

NICK. Is there no way to warn the men?

INNKEEPER. It's already too late. I fear the worse is about to happen.

NICK. We cannot stay here and do nothing. I am to fight.

THEY BOTH EXIT

ENTER THE GYPSY AND REVEREND

REVEREND. What brings you out on a night like this?

GYPSY. That's of no concern of yours, Reverend.

REVEREND. There are smugglers abroad.

GYPSY. So?

REVEREND. If the authorities find you wandering around the forest for no reason, they will connect you with tonight's happenings.

GYPSY. I have nothing to fear from the authorities.

REVEREND. What makes you so certain of that?

GYPSY. Let us say I have friends in high places.

REVEREND. How high?

GYPSY. Let us say the Magistrate of this parish and I have an understanding.

REVEREND. Is that where you have been this evening?

GYPSY. That is of no concern of yours.

REVEREND. I certainly hope you have not been to see the Magistrate.

GYPSY. And what if I have.

REVEREND. You obviously have not heard the news.

GYPSY. What news?

REVEREND. The Magistrate has been found dead. Shot through the head.

GYPSY. That cannot be so.

REVEREND. The authorities are looking for the last person who may have seen the Magistrate alive. He left my house earlier tonight and was never seen again.

THEY EXIT

TWO

ENTER THE INNKEEPER AND GYPSY

THE INNKEEPER BRINGS ON A DUCK STALL

INNKEEPER. We'll set up our stalls here. The King and his nobles are to visit the area. There's to be a fair in his honour.

GYPSY. Perhaps there will be a chance for us to entertain before the court?

INNKEEPER. It'll certainly be an opportune moment to earn a few bob. The first thing we do is double our prices. The King's followers can afford it.

GYPSY. If I play my hand right, I could become the King's consort.

INNKEEPER. Not if we don't get ourselves organised – and fast. I want you to set up by the entrance there. That way you gets them coming in and coming out.

GYPSY. And you – where will you set up?

INNKEEPER. Me? I shall set up over here. I want people to see my duck stall as soon as they enter the enclosure. Do we have everything?

GYPSY. I have my crystal ball – that is all I need.

INNKEEPER. Not at all. Today I want you to concentrate on dancing.

GYPSY. My art be fortune telling! It's what I do best.

INNKEEPER. Your art be in your exotic dancing. It's what pays the most.

GYPSY. Aye, and the rest.

INNKEEPER. If the paying customer wants to take you into the tent for a bit of company – then 'tis only right and proper.

GYPSY. It's not right and proper. Besides, what happens when my company be not worth the paying?

INNKEEPER. Then you can gaze into your crystal ball to your hearts content. Until then you play by the rules set out.

GYPSY. And you – are you content to stand by a duck stall handing out balls?

INNKEEPER. What of my balls?

GYPSY. You have a talent for more.

INNKEEPER. Enough of my talents. We both have livings to make.

GYPSY. There be more to life than making a living.

INNKEEPER. We are put on this earth to get by as best we can, and that's an end to it.

GYPSY. We are put on this earth for more noble matters, surely?

INNKEEPER. Not at all, unless you happen to be both noble in birth as well as in aspirations.

GYPSY. I'm not going to listen to any more of this.

INNKEEPER. Tell me, any more news of the Magistrate?

GYPSY. All I know is that he dined with the Reverend last night. As a storm was beginning to brew, the Magistrate decided to go home early. Once home, he went to bed and that was when the dreadful thing happened.

INNKEEPER. They say he was shot.

GYPSY. There is no doubt.

INNKEEPER. Perhaps the Magistrate took his own life.

GYPSY. The Magistrate was shot through the back of the head.

INNKEEPER. And what of the Excise Man?

GYPSY. He too is dead.

INNKEEPER. Two deaths in one night. The authorities will be keen to find the culprits.

GYPSY. They already suspect Nick Dawkins for the murder of the Excise Man.

INNKEEPER. You realise they will send a new Magistrate.

GYPSY. One who may not be so inclined to keep the inn open.

THE GYPSY EXITS

ENTER NICK

NICK. I must away from here, and quick!

INNKEEPER. But what of your family?

NICK. My family need me alive, not swinging from a tree. Besides, Jack can cope. He is my son, after all.

INNKEEPER. So you are to depart?

NICK. I can hide out in the forest first. I can then travel to another country. They say French women excel where it counts.

INNKEEPER. You will forever be on the run. Jumping from every shadow.

NICK. 'Tis the way of the world.

INNKEEPER. Why did you have to shoot at the Excise Man? You could have escaped easy enough.

NICK. The pistol mis-fired. 'Twas an accident.

INNKEEPER. You try telling the authorities that. They will want blood – your blood! If they capture you, you will be hung before the week is out.

NICK. Before I go, I must ask you a favour.

INNKEEPER. Ask away.

NICK. Jack, you must watch out for him. He's the only son I have.

INNKEEPER. I will do what I can.

NICK. I hear I am also accused of killing the Magistrate.

INNKEEPER. You appear to be a popular fellow amongst the authorities.

NICK. Who could possibly want to murder the Magistrate?

INNKEEPER. The list is as long as the shadows cast by the tallest of trees.

NICK EXITS, FOLLOWED BY THE INNKEEPER

ENTER GYPSY AND JACK

GYPSY. Roll up! Roll up! Come to the fair!

JACK. I used to love going to the fair. All them booths. All that noise and clutter. Shows. Strange animals. Dancing bears.

GYPSY. You shouldn't take on so. Your father will be all right.

JACK. But I feel so angry. Inside, my stomach feels like a knot.

GYPSY. Why not dance a gig with me? (*She sides up to him*)

JACK. I just feel it to be wrong to go to a fair when my father be on the run.

GYPSY. I know your father well. He would not want you to mope around like a sick dog.

JACK. My father be facing a rope if he be caught. What have we done to have this happen to us?

GYPSY. We have done nothing. It's an evil spirit playing sport with us.

JACK. I also have a mother who is distraught, yet I dandy around a fairground.

GYPSY. (*Looking around*) Look, the Innkeeper isn't around. Why not knock three ducks off his stand and win a prize for the lady of your life?

JACK. I don't know –

GYPSY. Do it! Vent your anger.

JACK. I'll do it! I can knock feathers off ducks!

JACK THROWS THREE BALLS AT THE DUCKS. HE KNOCKS THEM DOWN. THE GYPSY IS IMPRESSED

GYPSY. You're a great shot. (*She gives him a medal*) Here, take this fine medal. Give it to the girl of your dreams.

JACK. I will, surely. When I find her.

GYPSY. She may be nearer than you think.

JACK. I don't think so.

JACK EXITS

ENTER THE INNKEEPER

INNKEEPER. How goes business?

GYPSY. The fair is doing well enough.

INNKEEPER. And my duck stall?

GYPSY. These bark-dwellers are too skilled at hitting ducks off a stall. Even the doctor from London succeeded in winning a medal.

INNKEEPER. Not to worry. We still have a few shilling earned.

GYPSY. I'm glad to hear it.

INNKEEPER. And you – what of your trade?

GYPSY. Slow at first, but picking up.

INNKEEPER. So all your dark portends are failing to come true. Perhaps your crystal ball is in need of a polish?

GYPSY. My crystal ball serves me well enough. Some of the warnings be too subtle for common folk -

INNKEEPER. I see. If your insight be right, it's an amazing feat. If it be wrong, then it be too subtle for common folk. I fear you are picking the best of two worlds.

GYPSY. You can mock.

INNKEEPER. I'll let you know the truth of it later, when I count out the final takings. That be how I judge the success of any venture.

GYPSY. I know not why I stay with you. You never appreciate my skills and talents.

INNKEEPER. You cannot say that. I value your skills and talents beyond compare. 'Tis a shame you're not back in your booth practicing them on a paying public.

GYPSY. All right! I'm going!

INNKEEPER. (*Turns to the audience and shouts*) Roll up! Roll up! Take your chances! Three balls to knock three ducks off their arses!

THE INNKEEPER EXITS WITH THE DUCK STALL

ENTER THE DOCTOR

DOCTOR. Do you know, I always believed galleries to be fixed never to offer prizes. To think, I won a medal off the duck stand.

GYPSY. Let me see it.

DOCTOR. What's it worth to let you see it?

GYPSY. I know not your meaning.

DOCTOR. I'm sure it's worth a lie on the grass.

GYPSY. If you want a lie on the grass, then you pay like other customers.

DOCTOR. I'm a poor doctor. A quick five minutes isn't going to hurt.

GYPSY. A quick five minutes can do all the hurt in the world.

DOCTOR. You're safe enough with me.

GYPSY. Oh, really!

DOCTOR. I have a potion you can take.

GYPSY. And what if your potion fails to work. What if in nine months time –

DOCTOR. I shall return from London and make an honest woman of you.

GYPSY. I'll tell you what. I'll see to my business and you see to yours.

DOCTOR. I don't understand.

GYPSY. You have a right hand, don't you?

DOCTOR. I do.

GYPSY. Then use it.

DOCTOR. I shall take my trade elsewhere.

GYPSY. You do that.

THE DOCTOR EXITS

ENTER THE INKEEPER

A STORM IS BREWING

INNKEEPER. This storm is going to put a stop to further business today. We may as well pack up.

GYPSY. Maybe the storm will pass.

INNKEEPER. Trust the weather to spoil our attempts to shake these simpletons out of a few bob.

GYPSY. I dislike this place. This be a place where clocks fail to tick. A place where the water runs red on a full moon. A body only has to turn a corner to be confronted with visions not seen elsewhere in the world.

INNKEEPER. I've never heard such gibbering. Sometimes you push good fortune too far.

GYPSY. We've known each other a long time.

INNKEEPER. That still doesn't give you the right to preach – people like us have little choice in life. We continue as best we can.

GYPSY. And live a life full of poverty.

INNKEEPER. I don't understand you. You talk about leaving the forest but you stay. You hate the inn but you continue to work in it. You used to have an understanding with the Magistrate but you have nothing to show for it.

GYPSY. What does any woman have to show after being associated with a man?

INNKEEPER. Either a belly full of children or the pox.

THE GYPSY EXITS

ENTER QUIGLEY

INNKEEPER. Ah, Mistress Quigley. Tell me, are you really a witch? They say the forest be thick with witches – especially on wind-wracked nights like this.

QUIGLEY. Tonight be no different from many other.

INNKEEPER. The evening may begin well enough, then a sudden clap of thunder will come to shake the trees and chill the air.

QUIGLEY. I see you are well-versed in forest lore.

INNKEEPER. It's a night when strange creatures creep forth with their tongues hanging from their mouths in a frightened manner – that be dark forces at work in my book.

QUIGLEY. They do say the forest be thick with brainless idiots – not witches.

INNKEEPER. I must allow, you don't look much like a witch. You lack a witches beard.

QUIGLEY. I be a mere woman, with perhaps more wit than her neighbour – but nothing else.

INNKEEPER. Where's your broom?

QUIGLEY. I have none.

INNKEEPER. Where's your black cat?

QUIGLEY. I have no cat, black or other.

INNKEEPER. Are you not meant to sport a raven on your shoulder? An extra teat on your body to allow beasts to suck at will? Do you not mutter away and scold the world?

QUIGLEY. Why don't you go and play with yourself? And leave us women to converse with men of stature.

INNKEEPER. I have no need to play with myself – I have plenty of women to meet my needs.

QUIGLEY. But what if your needs were to shrivel into nothing? What then?

INNKEEPER. How can that happen? I am man enough for any woman.

QUIGLEY. Anything is possible in the forest.

QUIGLEY EXITS

ENTER THE DOCTOR

INNKEEPER. Good evening, doctor. I hope your room is to your satisfaction.

DOCTOR. I am looking for Mistress Quigley.

INNKEEPER. You've just missed her. Can I be of assistance?

DOCTOR. You realise that London is gripped by the plague.

INNKEEPER. I had heard.

DOCTOR. I understand that people here in the forest are beginning to die also.

INNKEEPER. People in the forest die from many causes.

DOCTOR. But not of the plague?

INNKEEPER. We have yet to enjoy that particular visitation.

DOCTOR. Then I am not too late.

INNKEEPER. Too late for what?

DOCTOR. We must do something before the plague takes a hold of the forest. In London, people are dying by the thousands. And there's nothing being done.

INNKEEPER. You could always try painting red crosses on peoples' doors.

DOCTOR. That doesn't do any good.

INNKEEPER. It may stop the plague from spreading. It certainly stops people from venturing abroad.

DOCTOR. So people have to lock themselves away to await death?

INNKEEPER. If there is nothing else to be done –

DOCTOR. But there is something to be done – I have a medicine –

INNKEEPER. Ah, now I understand. You wish to sell your potions to an unsuspecting public. I think you had better seek out Mistress Quigley. I'm sure she will be fascinated by your ideas.

THE DOCTOR EXITS

ENTER THE REVEREND

REVEREND. Ah, I thought I'd find you here.

INNKEEPER. How goes it, Reverend?

REVEREND. There is to be a hanging. Nick Dawkins has been captured. He stands convicted of a heinous crime.

INNKEEPER. The Excise Man was shot by accident. Nick has no reason to swing from the oak.

REVEREND. He was found guilty and now must be punished. It's the law.

INNKEEPER. What about forgiveness?

REVEREND. The law does not recognise forgiveness. The man stands condemned. We have to show an example. We cannot tolerate murder in the parish.

INNKEEPER. But the pistol fired premature.

REVEREND. It was aimed at a King's servant. There's nothing premature about that.

INNKEEPER. But he saw no harm in moving caskets from one barn to another. Many in these parts do it. It's common practice.

REVEREND. Enough of this prattle. The hanging is to begin.

ENTER NICK, CARRYING A NOOSE

INNKEEPER. I just pray he can face his fate with dignity. I pray the hangman sends him to hell will all the gentleness and science a man can muster.

REVEREND. I fear he is to die a slow, painful and bitter death.

INNKEEPER. May you rot in hell for such words.

REVEREND. I cannot alter the rule of law.

INNKEEPER. You can at least pray for the poor man's soul.

REVEREND. Look, the hanging is about to begin.

NICK HANGS HIMSELF. THERE IS THUNDER

THE REVEREND EXITS

ENTER ALICE. NICK REMAINS HANGING

ALICE. I've never seen a hanged man before.

INNKEEPER. Nobody should see such things.

ALICE. If we are to live in the forest then we must become accustomed to such sights.

INNKEEPER. The one does not follow the other.

ALICE. Will he be cut down?

INNKEEPER. You know we cannot.

THE THUNDER CRACKS

ALICE. But the sky is about to open. He will be wracked in the storm – shafted asunder by lightning.

INNKEEPER. You know we're not allowed to remove the body. It must remain hanging. We must depart, never to return.

ALICE. The law will pay dear for this foul deed.

INNKEEPER. We cannot take on the law and hope to win. Many have tried and failed.

ALICE. Then what are we to do?

INNKEEPER. The best we can aim for is a continuation of the trade. *(He rubs himself)* Nick knew the risks of running with the contraband.

ALICE. What ails you?

INNKEEPER. I know not.

ALICE. Why do you rub yourself in such a manner?

INNKEEPER. 'Tis no matter.

ALICE. I, too, have been unwell of late. I often have the fever, but it passes, it always does.

INNKEEPER. Go, you must depart from here.

ALICE EXITS

ENTER THE REVEREND

REVEREND. *(Looking at Nick)* He wouldn't call for me.

INNKEEPER. You should have gone to him nevertheless.

REVEREND. Perhaps.

INNKEEPER. How is Alice?

REVEREND. She is fine.

INNKEEPER. Are you certain of that?

REVEREND. She is starting to pine for the outside world. I sometimes fear for her health. She is often poorly, listless. Ever since her mother died -

INNKEEPER. Is there any news on the Magistrates murder?

REVEREND. None. He had many enemies, many of which were out free trading on the night he died.

INNKEEPER. Is there no clue then?

REVEREND. His death was not exactly premature. It would appear he was not long for this world. If a bullet hadn't dispatched him, natural causes would have been the death of him before long.

INNKEEPER. Natural causes?

REVEREND. He had a fatal ailment. On closer inspection, he would not have lasted out a year.

INNKEEPER. So, the murderer was impatient.

REVEREND. Ignorant, more like.

THE REVEREND EXITS

Murder Mysteries Vol 1

ENTER QUIGLEY

QUIGLEY. *(Looking at Nick)* I see you are fascinated by the dead. Especially when they dangle from a hanging tree.

INNKEEPER. You must away from here.

QUIGLEY. I will not!

INNKEEPER. Away, I say!

QUIGLEY. They do say I be a poor species of woman, well past my prime and obliged to use Satan's power to steal men's affections - *(she looks up at Nick)* be they alive or dead.

INNKEEPER. You leave him alone! He has to remain on the rope – a severe reminder to anyone considering a breach of the law.

QUIGLEY. I daresay he be wanting to come down off the gallows. Perhaps that can be arranged. I wouldn't ask for much in return.

INNKEEPER. You cannot interfere! You must depart! You and your kind are not welcome! You never were and 'twill be a long time before you ever will be! So, be on your way, witch!

QUIGLEY. The gentleman here don't mind my company.

INNKEEPER. You leave him be!

QUIGLEY. *(Addressing Nick)* I can let thee down. It wouldn't take much. I have the art to free thee from thy bond. I can make walking the earth a possible action again.

INNKEEPER. You cannot! He is dead. He must remain so. He cannot be allowed to roam free.

QUIGLEY. You can do nothing to stop me. He be a soul in torment. Freeing him will ease the pain. Here, go ahead, set thyself free. Venture once more into the forest.

INNKEEPER. No! I won't allow it!

QUIGLEY. Escape. It can be done.

INNKEEPER. Noooo!

THEY EXIT

THREE

ENTER THE INNKEEPER AND GYPSY. GYPSY IS CARRYING A PARCEL

GYPSY. We're wasting our time here. These people don't want what we're offering. They'd rather sit and watch the leaves grow on the trees.

INNKEEPER. You're not happy unless you're complaining about something. Now, get that contraband shifted, and quickly!

THE INNKEEPER EXITS AS THE REVEREND ENTERS

REVEREND. What's this, a travelling gypsy? Be off with you, before I call the constable.

GYPSY. I'm merely trying to make a simple honest living, sir.

REVEREND. I know well enough of your living. It is neither simple or honest. So, begone!

GYPSY. You have yet to see what I have to offer.

REVEREND. Offer?

GYPSY. 'Tis the finest tea.

REVEREND. Where has this tea come from?

GYPSY. It's not for me to comment.

REVEREND. It's smuggled, is it not?

GYPSY. I cannot say.

REVEREND. This is an absolute disgrace.

GYPSY. Will you not take the tea then?

REVEREND. I will not! Now, begone!

THE REVEREND EXITS

ENTER ALICE

ALICE. Was that my father I saw?

GYPSY. It was.

ALICE. What did he want?

GYPSY. Nothing. I offered him some tea.

ALICE. Did he accept it?

GYPSY. He did not.

ALICE. Why not?

GYPSY. He said it was smuggled.

ALICE. I am bored. I keep getting headaches. I don't seem to be able to settle to anything.

GYPSY. Then you can help me sell this tea.

ALICE. I am to leave this place.

GYPSY. And where would you go?

ALICE. London.

GYPSY. And die of the plague?

ALICE. It would be better than staying here dying of boredom.

GYPSY. If you are bored then join your father in some charity work.

ALICE. I'm not that bored!

GYPSY. You remind me of your mother, you know. She was always restless.

ALICE. I didn't know you knew my mother.

GYPSY. There is plenty you know nothing of.

ALICE EXITS

ENTER THE INNKEEPER

INNKEEPER. The authorities are still on to us, ever since that Excise Man got shot. Not to mention the murder of the Magistrate *(He looks around)* This be the place it all happened, you know.

GYPSY. Every tree in the forest is able to tell a sad tale.

INNKEEPER. Nick was a good man. It truly was an accident. The pistol fired by mistake. We live in terrible times, skulking around the place like frightened rabbits.

GYPSY. It's the way of the forest.

INNKEEPER. I know it to be true, it's knowing it to be right I find hard to swallow. Where be the justice in all this pain?

GYPSY. I know not. It's too deep for me to fathom.

INNKEEPER. At least we are about to continue the trade.

GYPSY. Is that wise?

INNKEEPER. What is wisdom against such conditions under which we live?

GYPSY. There are rumours of a plague.

INNKEEPER. A few people have been taken ill, nothing more.

GYPSY. A plague is all we need.

INNKEEPER. I wonder how the doctor from London is getting on?

GYPSY. He is bound to put Mistress Quigley in a foul temper. She will not take kindly to others doctoring the sick.

INNKEEPER. *(Scratching himself)* Talking of doctoring, I have been itching awful recently.

GYPSY. Most probably an old dose of the pox.

INNKEEPER. Caught from you perhaps. God alone knows who've you've been with recently – it certainly hasn't been me.

GYPSY. Get lost!

GYPSY EXITS

ENTER THE DOCTOR

INNKEEPER. I think you should depart from the forest.

DOCTOR. On what basis?

INNKEEPER. You interfere. You draw attention to yourself.

DOCTOR. How can a simple doctor draw attention to himself?

INNKEEPER. There is business here. You disturb our work.

DOCTOR. You're a free trader. A venturer of the night.

INNKEEPER. I wouldn't ask too many questions if I were you.

DOCTOR. I don't understand. We're both working men trying to make our way in the world.

INNKEEPER. (*Doubles in pain*) Damn this affliction!

DOCTOR. If I didn't know better, I would say something was ailing you.

INNKEEPER. Nothing that you can fix. Now be off with you.

DOCTOR. I tried to cure the Magistrate, you know.

INNKEEPER. Oh, when?

DOCTOR. On the night he was murdered.

INNKEEPER. What business had you with the Magistrate?

DOCTOR. Medical.

INNKEEPER. How so, medical?

DOCTOR. Let us say he may have had a disease of a personal nature. That he may have wanted a potion for it. That it may have been a long standing illness.

THE DOCTOR EXITS

ENTER ALICE

ALICE. I wish my father in hell!

INNKEEPER. What ails him this time?

ALICE. He is against my coming here.

INNKEEPER. He most probably thinks my inn to be a den of vice.

ALICE. But I am old enough to make my own decisions.

INNKEEPER. It wouldn't do to cross him too much. He has a strong influence in the forest. The wrath of the church I can do without.

ALICE. But he takes too much on himself.

INNKEEPER. He cares for you as any father should. I daresay he worries.

ALICE. Ever since mother died –

INNKEEPER. Bear with him. At least for the time being. But for now, you must depart.

ALICE. But I want to help you.

INNKEEPER. You cannot. There might be danger. Now go.

ALICE. There is something between you and my father.

INNKEEPER. We have different views on the world, that is all. Your father thinks innkeeping to be an occupation for devil worshipers.

ALICE. No, it is more than that.

INNKEEPER. Not a bit of it. Now, please. Go.

ALICE. Why will nobody in this forest take my views into account? 'Tis enough to suffer physical pain without all this mental anguish as well.

INNKEEPER. What physical pain?

ALICE. 'Tis nothing. I have been ailing for the past year now. I know not what it is.

ALICE EXITS

ENTER JACK

THE INNKEEPER CONTINUES TO RUB HIMSELF

JACK. What's the matter with you?

INNKEEPER. Nothing.

THE INNKEEPER HANDS JACK A COSH

JACK. What's this?

INNKEEPER. You know what to do. As soon as the doctor returns to his room, let him have it.

JACK. Are you sure he'll be off his guard?

INNKEEPER. He'll be off his guard.

JACK. What do we do with him then?

INNKEEPER. Drag him outside. We'll get rid of him later. *(There is a faint bell. Jack listens)* What's the matter with you?

JACK. Can't you hear it?

INNKEEPER. Hear what?

JACK. I don't know, do I? A bell of some sort.

INNKEEPER. You're being ridiculous.

JACK. (*Shudders*) And this feeling – a cold feeling. Down my spine.

INNKEEPER. You're imagining things. Now, get on with it.

JACK. What makes you so sure the doctor's carrying valuables anyway? Suppose he's carrying nothing but medicine.

INNKEEPER. Stop complaining, will you? You have work to do.

JACK EXITS

ENTER A GHOSTLY NICK

NICK HAS A ROPE AROUND HIS NECK

INNKEEPER. What's going on?

NICK. Come on lads! Get a move on with those barrels! And keep the noise down! We don't want the revenue men to catch us.

INNKEEPER. Nick? Is that you?

NICK. What we need is a few horses. That would make our lives a lot easier.

INNKEEPER. I don't believe any of this!

NICK. You haven't got the odd horse, have you? A cart wouldn't go amiss either. We'll make it worth your while.

INNKEEPER. I think I want to leave.

NICK. Suit yourself. We'll move the barrels by hand. *(a storm erupts)* Come on, lads.

INNKEEPER. Nick, speak to me.

NICK. If you know what's good for you, return to your hearth. There's to be blood spilt tonight.

INNKEEPER. What do you mean, "blood spilt tonight"?

NICK EXITS FOLLOWED BY A BEWILDERED INNKEEPER

ENTER THE GYPSY AND REVEREND

GYPSY. Any further news on the Magistrate?

REVEREND. One prays his soul is in heaven.

GYPSY. I mean on the investigation of his death.

REVEREND. There are plenty of suspects. We may never know who the real culprit is.

GYPSY. They say the Magistrate had the pox.

REVEREND. I don't think we can blame the plague for his demise.

GYPSY. I didn't mean the plague.

REVEREND. I cannot linger any longer. I must away.

GYPSY. I understand you were the last to see him alive.

REVEREND. Except for the murderer, of course.

GYPSY. Unless the two are one and the same.

REVEREND. I refuse to listen to such idle speculation.

THE REVEREND EXITS

ENTER THE DOCTOR

DOCTOR. You must excuse me. I must away from here.

GYPSY. Why the haste?

DOCTOR. This place be not safe for mortal men.

GYPSY. But I thought you came here to administer the sick.

DOCTOR. I deal with the bodily sick. Here, people be sick in the mind.

GYPSY. It's a shame you couldn't help the Magistrate.

DOCTOR. Why do you mention the Magistrate?

GYPSY. I understand he sought you out.

DOCTOR. He wanted my advice, certainly.

GYPSY. What about?

DOCTOR. A medical matter.

GYPSY. He had the pox.

DOCTOR. He had the pox bad. It was destroying his brain.

GYPSY. Such ailments come and go.

DOCTOR. What the Magistrate had was far more serious. It was the sort that can be passed from one generation to another.

GYPSY. Why should that concern the Magistrate? He was without family.

DOCTOR. That's not what he told me.

GYPSY. I don't understand.

DOCTOR. I cannot say any more. I must pack my belongings and be gone.

GYPSY. You must tell me everything you know.

THE DOCTOR EXITS

ENTER THE INNKEEPER, IN A DAZE

GYPSY. Boss? Are you all right?

INNKEEPER. This is truly a curious place. I know not what's happening.

GYPSY. I have decided. It is time we went our separate ways.

INNKEEPER. You cannot leave me, it's disloyal.

GYPSY. I started life with nothing, 'tis fitting I end it the same way.

INNKEEPER. How so?

GYPSY. A poor single woman against an evil harsh world. Shunned from every threshold in the land.

INNKEEPER. You need me for safety and protection.

GYPSY. You couldn't safety and protect yourself against the rain –

INNKEEPER. It's not true.

GYPSY. Ours is like many such ventures. It begins bright and shiny enough – but soon dulls, like a new penny in a beggar's pocket.

INNKEEPER. You're being fanciful – 'tisn't fitting for a tinker to string such poetic words together.

GYPSY. There was a time you would turn a neat phrase yourself before setting it to music.

INNKEEPER. (*Hardens*) I do not care to hear of such talk.

GYPSY. You never care to hear of any sort of talk.

INNKEEPER. There's no point to it.

GYPSY. I don't understand you at all. We used to be so close.

INNKEEPER. We are two people working together. Our partnership is merely that, a partnership. An arrangement.

GYPSY. Except when the nights be cold.

INNKEEPER. That's nothing more than convenience. Two people can keep warmer together than apart.

GYPSY. You will always be cold, inside and out.

INNKEEPER. It's my decision.

GYPSY. So be it. I must away. It's getting dark, no time to be out in the forest.

INNKEEPER. Are you serious about giving up our partnership?

GYPSY. I am determined.

INNKEEPER. But we arrived in this forest together, many years ago.

GYPSY. Much against my better judgement.

INNKEEPER. Then we have a duty to depart the same way.

GYPSY. You be a fool.

INNKEEPER. We all be fools in the forest. This place makes dolts out of scholars.

GYPSY (*Looking around*) I have always felt uneasy about this place. I have told you often, but you have always refused to listen.

INNKEEPER. I will listen now.

GYPSY. Now is too late.

INNKEEPER. Now is never too late. Let us leave this place together. Once we have the sun on our heads we will be able to think clearly.

GYPSY. But what of the future?

INNKEEPER. What future?

GYPSY. You and I, we have not been right together. Ever since you stopped writing ballads –

INNKEEPER. Why do you do it? Why do you go on about the past? Has it never occurred to you why I stopped writing ballads?

GYPSY. No.

INNKEEPER. There is nothing to write for. *I* have nothing to write for. Ballads are for people secure in the world.

GYPSY. Then make yourself secure.

INNKEEPER. That is easier said than done.

GYPSY. Let us leave this place. Let us find a place where you can sing for your supper.

INNKEEPER. But I have no instrument to play. (*The Gypsy fetches an instrument which she hands to the Innkeeper*) How long have you had this?

GYPSY. Long enough.

INNKEEPER. I threw it away.

GYPSY. I retrieved it.

INNKEEPER. I'm not sure I can play.

THE GYPSY EXITS

GHOSTLY SOUND EFFECTS

ENTER NICK WHO CROSSES THE STAGE

ENTER THE REVEREND WHO JOINS THE INNKEEPER

REVEREND. I am a man of God. I do not allow myself to be taken in by such fanciful notions.

INNKEEPER. And I am an innkeeper. I thought having a ghost on the premises would be good for business, but 'tis not so. The last thing I want is spirits entering my premises as bold as brass, disturbing my guests and frightening away trade. Do you understand me?

REVEREND. Perhaps your ghost was a simple intruder.

INNKEEPER. He had a noose around his neck.

REVEREND. There's no accounting for strange behaviour.

INNKEEPER. Will you take me seriously?

REVEREND. And did he speak, this man? Did you recognise him?

INNKEEPER. Of course I recognised him. He wanted me to send him to hell with all the gentleness and science I could muster. He then cried out in agony and begged me to pull his boots and hasten his end.

REVEREND. I have read books, of course. But my experience of such matters is limited.

INNKEEPER. So, what's to be done then?

REVEREND. You already know my opinions on such matters. It's against the law of God. We dabble in matters of which we know nothing. What you propose is both wrong and sinful.

INNKEEPER. According to whom?

REVEREND. According to God.

INNKEEPER. So you refuse?

REVEREND. I refuse.

INNKEEPER. After what we have between us?

THE REVEREND AND INNKEEPER EXIT

ENTER GYPSY AND ALICE

ALICE. I have searched everywhere. The body cannot be found.

GYPSY. He cannot disappear. It's not natural.

ALICE. But the hanging tree be empty. Nothing hangs from the branch.

GYPSY. Perhaps he was taken down by a Christian traveller and given a decent burial.

ALICE. Perhaps he be taken by an evil and savage beast – the forest do house such creatures.

GYPSY. If we mean to live in the forest, we must be as cunning as the fox and as swift as the deer.

ALICE. But both the fox and deer become snarled in time and do die a miserable death.

GYPSY. We must return to the village. It's getting cold. *(The wind blows up)* The wind is beginning to rise. Wait.

ALICE. What is it?

GYPSY. Can't you feel it?

ALICE. I can feel nothing.

GYPSY. It's like a chill. It's like stumbling into a dark dank cave. And the wind, it's like a hot gale from hell itself. *(The wind drops)* It's gone. Whatever it was, it vanished as quickly as it appeared. *(The Gypsy looks at Alice)* Didn't you feel it? No, of course you didn't. That's because we failed to touch it. We were near, but still too far away. Yet it still touched us. Cold fingers gripped and stopped the blood from flowing into our hearts. I have decided, I am to depart this place.

ALICE. If you are to depart, then I must join you. I wish to see the world.

GYPSY. What does your father think to such an adventure?

ALICE. Being a reverend, my father has his mind on higher matters.

GYPSY. Surely you have a duty to honour his calling?

ALICE. I be my own person. Besides, I can pay. I have money.

THEY EXIT

ENTER THE INNKEEPER AND JACK

THE INNKEEPER IS CARRYING A KNIFE AND A DEAD RABBIT

INNKEEPER. Go and dispatch the good doctor. He has outlived his usefulness.

JACK. I will not do it. I will not add another killing to this sorry story.

INNKEEPER. Then leave me to attend my own business.

JACK. But this business of yours is foolhardy.

INNKEEPER. I still have to try it. It's my only hope.

JACK. It's a stupid thing to attempt.

INNKEEPER. They say killing a rabbit on a full moon and spreading the blood on the infected parts can cause miracles.

JACK. You would be better to spread the blood on your head – it's your brain that has shrunk, not your manhood.

INNKEEPER. My manhood gets smaller with every day that passes. At first I thought it was nothing, but that witch woman has spelled me good and proper.

JACK. Mistress Quigley is not a witch.

INNKEEPER. Examine me and you will see what I mean.

JACK. I don't think I need to do that. Get the Gypsy woman to examine you. She is far better equipped to give an opinion.

INNKEEPER. I cannot ask a woman that sort of question.

JACK. The Gypsy loves you for what you be, not what you carry in your breeches.

INNKEEPER. That is kind talk. I want to be with a woman, not a sister.

JACK. Then I must away. I will have nothing to do with sorcery.

INNKEEPER. Then away. I care not anymore.

JACK EXITS

ENTER QUIGLEY

INNKEEPER. Ah, Witch. Enough of this game-playing, undo the spell. And do it immediate.

QUIGLEY. I be not a witch. I am merely an old woman attempting to go about her business.

INNKEEPER. You are well known in the forest. People cross the path when you approach. Good honest folk dare not look you in the eye for fear of going blind. So you must undo your spell upon me, you rotten hag! Return me to normal!

QUIGLEY. No mortal being can cast spells.

INNKEEPER. You lie! Undress me and you will see a difference in my appearance. It's not natural.

QUIGLEY. I haven't had such an offer in years, for which I thank you.

INNKEEPER. I need to stand erect. You must oblige me. I have asked you, pleaded with you.

QUIGLEY. And now you threaten me?

INNKEEPER. I will not tarry with you any longer. Undo your spell and all will be well.

QUIGLEY. And if I don't?

INNKEEPER. You know the answer to that.

QUIGLEY. And if I cannot?

INNKEEPER. The same fate.

QUIGLEY. I have already spoken. The spell lives in your mind, it's not of my doing.

INNKEEPER. You think I jest, old woman.

QUIGLEY. On the contrary, I believe you to take such a small matter too much to heart.

INNKEEPER. Undo the spell!

QUIGLEY. You must do as you please.

INNKEEPER. I shall! (*The Innkeeper stabs her*) May your mother rue the day she dragged you screaming into the world.

HE DRAGS HER OFF

THE INNKEEPER RETURNS AS THE REVEREND ENTERS

REVEREND. I have looked everywhere for her.

INNKEEPER. *(Alarmed)* Who?

REVEREND. Alice.

INNKEEPER. She cannot have gone far.

REVEREND. She was talking of leaving the forest.

INNKEEPER. Perhaps she is right to do so.

REVEREND. How can you say that?

INNKEEPER. She has to find her own way in the world.

REVEREND. But she is my niece. Her place is by my side. And I fear for her life.

THE REVEREND STARTS TO COUGH

INNKEEPER. What ails you?

REVEREND. I feel ill. I feel hot and feverish.

INNKEEPER. You had better get home to bed.

THEY EXIT

ENTER THE GYPSY AND ALICE

GYPSY. You must help your father! He's ill!

ALICE. He has the plague. No one dare touch him.

GYPSY. But he's the Reverend of this parish.

ALICE. He's still a man dying of the plague.

GYPSY. How can you leave him so?

ALICE. May God have mercy on his soul. There is nothing more I can say or do.

GYPSY. But what if he dies? Who is to arrange his burial?

ALICE. Nobody. If he has the plague then he will be infectious.

GYPSY. So what is to be done?

ALICE. If you are that concerned for his welfare, then you must bury him yourself.

GYPSY. I cannot –

ALICE. Then just cover him with a sack. The rats will soon finish him off.

GYPSY. Cover him in a sack! What sort of niece can treat a father so?

ALICE. A niece who is to leave this place.

ALICE EXITS

ENTER THE INNKEEPER. HE IS ILL

GYPSY. Boss, is that you? What's the matter?

INNKEEPER. I'm cold. I have a chill.

GYPSY. We'll soon have you right.

INNKEEPER. I've had enough of this place. We must go. (*He collapses*)

GYPSY. How long have you been ailing like this?

INNKEEPER. God, am I thirsty.

GYPSY. Let me feel your head. (*She does so*) You're burning up. It's the forest fever. I must get you that London doctor.

INNKEEPER. He has departed.

GYPSY. Then I shall fetch Mistress Quigley.

INNKEEPER. She too has departed. There's not a doctor within miles – not one willing to help. Not one we can afford. And certainly not one that would attend someone riddled with the plague.

GYPSY. But I cannot leave you like this.

INNKEEPER. You must leave me to die in peace. It may already be too late for you.

GYPSY. But I cannot. You are my man.

INNKEEPER. If you don't get away, you'll catch the fever. You must save yourself.

GYPSY. Rest, we can talk later. (*She tries to make him comfortable*) Don't give up. We've been through far too much to be beaten now. I cannot allow the forest to take you away like this. I'll fight you every inch of the way.

INNKEEPER. You were always a fighter.

GYPSY. I must speak to you.

INNKEEPER. What about?

GYPSY. I need to confess.

INNKEEPER. You had better go and fetch the Reverend.

GYPSY. I need to confess to someone who will forgive me.

INNKEEPER. Forgive you, for what?

GYPSY. The Magistrate –

INNKEEPER. You surely have nothing to do with the Magistrate's death?

GYPSY. The Magistrate threatened to close down the inn.

INNKEEPER. Hardly a reason for murder. Besides, I thought you wanted us to leave this place.

GYPSY. But we had an understanding. A bond between us.

INNKEEPER. What bond?

GYPSY. Alice.

INNKEEPER. What of Alice?

GYPSY. She's the Magistrates's daughter.

INNKEEPER. I know.

GYPSY. You know.

INNKEEPER. Alice's mother told me. Just before she died. She made me take a pledge. I was to look after Alice as best I could. I loved Alice's mother, I would have done anything for her.

GYPSY. I had an agreement with the Magistrate. He was never to close down the inn as a price for my silence.

INNKEEPER. And the Magistrate turned against his agreement.

GYPSY. He was dying. He wanted to make amends. He wanted to speak to Alice.

INNKEEPER. And you killed him for that.

GYPSY. Not only for that, no. The Magistrate had the pox. It spread though the generations. Alice is already showing signs. I, too am infected.

INNKEEPER. So you went to the Magistrate's house.

GYPSY. I did. I executed my revenge. *(She takes out her pistol)* I told you the forest was a dangerous place.

A GUN FIRES OFF STAGE

INNKEEPER. What's that? 'Tis a pistol shot.

GYPSY. (*Addresses the audience*) If you know what's good for you, return to your hearth. There's to be blood spilled tonight.

THE INNKEEPER AND GYPSY EXIT

FINAL SCREAM

END OF PLAY

UNLUCKY FOR SOME

By

John Dunne

Characters
Inspector Frisby
Lewis Hayward
Margaret Hayward
Sarah Hayward
Annie Hill
Bert Hill
Charlie Hill
Mrs Ingleby
Major White

Set in a small country town at the turn of the 20th century,
a murder is committed, then another, then another. Will
Inspector Frisby solve the pile up of bodies?

ONE

THERE IS A GUNSHOT. ENTER INSPECTOR FRISBY AND LEWIS HAYWARD

FRISBY. Ladies and gentlemen. Do not be alarmed. My name is Inspector Frisby.

LEWIS. Inspector. What on earth's happened?

FRISBY. There has a been a murder. A Mr George Ingleby.

LEWIS. George Ingleby?

FRISBY. Do you know him?

LEWIS. He's a fellow trader in the town.

FRISBY. And you, sir. Who might you be?

LEWIS. My name's Hayward. Lewis Hayward.

FRISBY. And what is your occupation?

LEWIS. The same as George Ingleby. Photographer.

FRISBY. How long have you been a photographer in the town?

LEWIS. My wife and I arrived here in 1907. From Portsmouth.

FRISBY. Why did you move from Portsmouth?

LEWIS. Aldershot's a good place to raise a family. And it's nearer London. We're now well into a new century, Inspector, this is going to be our century.

FRISBY. Not a view held by Mr Ingleby.

LEWIS. Not any more, certainly.

FRISBY. You say you are married, Mr Hayward?

LEWIS. I am indeed. I have a wife, Margaret, and a young daughter, Sarah. My wife's just given birth. Another little girl. Alice.

FRISBY. Congratulations.

LEWIS. I'm not sure if my wife agrees. She's become a suffragette, I'm afraid. She thinks if this new century is going to achieve anything, its going to stop women falling pregnant every time their husbands smile at them.

FRISBY. We can expect a lot from the twentieth century, but that's asking too much.

LEWIS. My wife would like to work, but with a small baby – the most she can do is help me in my studio. Now, if you'll excuse me –

FRISBY. Certainly, Mr Hayward. I have to speak to a Annie Hill.

LEWIS. What on earth for?

FRISBY. I don't know. It just says so in my script.

LEWIS EXITS

ENTER ANNIE

ANNIE. Hello, I hope you don't mind my popping in. The name's Annie, Annie Hill. We live nearby. Bert and I. Bert's my husband. He's the head gardener for the town council – the only gardener, actually. We saw you arrive, Inspector. Just wondered if you needed any help - what with the dreadful deed and all.

FRISBY. And you? What do you do?

ANNIE. I'm chief cook and bottle washer –general skivvy, more like.

FRISBY. What about children?

ANNIE. Inspector! I hardly know you!

FRISBY. Do you have any children?

ANNIE. A lad. Charlie.

FRSIBY. Does he work here also?

ANNIE. When he can shift his backside. He helps Bert – my husband.

FRISBY. So, what do you know about this George Ingleby chap?

ANNIE. He's got a shop in the town. He's been here for years.

FRISBY. How did he react when Mr Hayward set up business?

ANNIE. Ingleby weren't too well pleased, I can tell you.

FRISBY. Surely he was able to handle a bit of healthy competition?

ANNIE. A lot of people are keen on this photography lark around here.

FRISBY. I hear in London, they go in for naughty postcards.

ANNIE. How do you mean, naughty?

FRISBY. Naked ladies.

ANNIE. Well, I'm not exposing my body parts for anyone. Not even Bert gets to see my private bits these days.

FRISBY. You have to keep abreast with what's happening in the world, that's what I always say.

ANNIE. The only breast we have to keep is the ones to feed our babies with.

FRISBY. There's more to life than feeding babies, you know.

ANNIE. You don't want to let my Bert hear you say that. He reckons women have far too many opinions as it is, it ain't good for them.

FRISBY. It sounds like your Bert wants to drag himself into the twentieth century.

ANNIE. If you'll excuse me. I can't stand here gossiping all day.

FRISBY. Not at all. I must speak to *(Checks his notes)* A Margaret Hayward.

ANNIE EXITS

ENTER MARGARET (SHE IS LUGGING A CARDBOARD HORSE)

FRISBY. What on earth is that?

MARGARET. It's a new idea of my husbands.

FRISBY. Go on, amaze me.

MARGARET. What do you think's our biggest earner?

FRISBY. Photographing people?

MARGARET. And what do they wear?

FRISBY. I imagine they wear their finery –

MARGARET. And where do you imagine we put these fine figures of photographic splendour?

FRISBY. In the studio. By the rubber plant – I don't know.

MARGARET. My husband plans to put them on horses. They'll look splendid on horses.

FRISBY. And where on earth are you going to get horses from?

MARGARET. Nowhere. We make them. We make the horses, take the photographs and paste them on the mounts – particularly popular amongst the army personnel stationed in the town.

FRISBY. It will never take on.

MARGARET. That's where you're wrong. It's already taken on. It's all the rage in London.

FRISBY. So, a customer comes in, asks to have his photo taken –

MARGARET. And we offer a range of exotic locations plus a choice of horses. The customer goes away supremely satisfied.

FRISBY. I suppose you could have horses standing bolt upright. Horses galloping. Horses jumping over fences. White horses, dark horses. You can have more than one horse for group poses. I've seen pictures of the Wright Brothers fabulous flying machine – you can have people sitting in aeroplanes. Can you imagine it, areoplanes flying over Aldershot. *(Looking at her horse)* Mind you, you could make the horses smaller.

MARGARET. Excuse me, don't you have a murder to investigate?

FRISBY. Oh yes, poor Mr Ingleby.

MARGARET. Where did he die?

FRISBY. In his studio. It would seem he was working – alone.

MARGARET. Perhaps it was suicide. He was getting rather depressed lately.

FRISBY. He was shot in the back of the head.

MARGARET. What a dreadful business. I wonder how his dear wife is coping?

FRISBY. I am about to interview her.

MARGARET EXITS

ENTER MRS INGLEBY

FRISBY. Mrs Ingleby. Do come in. How are you, my dear woman?

INGLEBY. *(Looks at the horse)* Someone told me they saw Mrs Hayward dragging a horse into here.

FRISBY. Is nothing private in Aldershot?

INGLEBY. I don't know what the Hayward's are doing here anyway. They've been in Aldershot a year now and during that time they have attempted to put my husband out of business.

FRISBY. How so?

INGLEBY. My husband is – was - a photographer.

FRISBY. As, indeed, is Mr Hayward.

INGLEBY. No, sir, Mr Hayward is a fake, a fraud. I don't know what possessed the Haywards to move from Portsmouth in the first place. They did nothing but harm my husband's trade. Hayward's just an upstart. A trickster.

FRISBY. But Hayward appears to be a fake who is making money. A fraud who has more work than he can handle. A trickster who has customers recommending other customers. Surely there was enough trade for both men to enjoy.

INGLEBY. Hayward's not interested in trade. He's only interested in theatricals. Gimmicks. Illusions.

FRISBY. Photography is an illusion – and much more besides.

INGLEBY. We had hoped he would have seen reason –

FRISBY. And do what? Leave Aldershot? Go elsewhere?

INGLEBY. If he have a shred of common decency –

FRISBY. Lewis Hayward has a family to feed. I don't think common decency comes into it.

INGLEBY. So, you're not going to arrest Hayward?

FRISBY. On what grounds?

INGLEBY. On the grounds that he hated my husband.

FRISBY. It sounds like your husband had more grounds to hate Hayward.

INGLEBY. Instead it's my husband who has been murdered, Inspector.

FRISBY. Was nobody with your husband when he died, Mrs Ingleby?

INGLEBY. He had people around during the evening. They played a few games of cards, but they all left early. My husband then went into his studio to work. The next thing we know -

FRISBY. This game of cards – who was there, exactly?

INGLEBY. That, I don't know, Inspector.

MRS INGLEBY EXITS

ENTER CHARLIE

CHARLIE. Perhaps I should join the army. I think I'd look dashing in a uniform.

FRISBY. And you are?

CHARLIE. The name's Hill, Charlie Hill.

FRISBY. You're too young to join up, surely? What if there's a war?

CHARLIE. Then I'll go and fight.

FRISBY. Then you'll be killed.

CHARLIE. Then I'll die a hero.

FRISBY. You'll die a fool.

CHARLIE. Besides, there's not going to be a war.

FRISBY. Then why join the army?

CHARLES. I want a few bob in my pocket, that's why.

FRISBY. Haven't you got a job then?

CHARLES. I help my old man do the gardening around here. But he pays next to nothing. All I want to do is join the other lads. Go to the pub. Go to the town hall dance. Get off with all the girls.

FRISBY. Not all the girls, I hope. I expect some of the girls in Aldershot to have a sense of decency.

CHARLIE. Aye, but a lot don't. A lot are taken in by a few bob. And what with so many soldiers around the place, us local lads have no chance.

FRISBY. Some of the girls who hang around here are not the kind of girls for you - take my word for it. Three minutes pleasure and you'll be tied to them for the rest of your life. Is that what you want?

CHARLIE. Oh, and what is the kind of girl for me?

FRISBY. Someone smarter than the rest. Someone who sees a life free from the drudgery of childbirth and poverty. Somebody who wants to embrace the twentieth century and make it her century. Someone who doesn't want to go behind the pub with her drawers in her handbag.

CHARLIE. So where on earth is a poor country lad to find such a person?

FRISBY. Don't worry. Someone will turn up. Now, I must ask you a few questions about George Ingleby. This card game of his -

CHARLIE. I know nothing about George Ingleby. We didn't move in the same circles. Please, excuse me.

FRISBY. Not at all. *(Checking his notes)* I must speak to a Major White.

CHARLIE EXITS

ENTER MAJOR WHITE

MAJOR. Excuse me, was that Charlie Hill I saw running off?

FRISBY. Who wants to know?

MAJOR. My name's White, Major - Retired. I also happen to be a town council member. I also own Highview Manor – for my sins.

FRISBY. I'm Inspector Frisby. I'm trying to investigate the murder of one George Ingleby.

MAJOR. Poor Ingleby. If I can help in any way?

FRISBY. Did you know Mr Ingleby?

MAJOR. Of course I knew him. He used to do all the photography for us in the town. Weddings, that sort of caper.

FRISBY. Used to?

MAJOR. Until friend Hayward came along. It all started when I got a complaint from Ingleby about Lewis Hayward. He was stealing the chap's business, don't you know. As a local personage in the area, I agreed to go and speak to Hayward. But the chap was busy. I spoke to his wife, Margaret, instead. A damned handsome woman, wouldn't you agree?

FRISBY. Go on.

MAJOR. Well, she told me her husband had been selling naughty postcards to the army chaps billoted hereabouts. Well, I was shocked to the core, I can tell you.

FRISBY. And was he – selling naughty postcards?

MAJOR. The filly was having me on. She said that was why they had to leave Portsmouth. She told me her husband would take intimate photographs of her and sell then for a shilling each to the sailors. I realised immediately she was one of these free thinking women.

FRISBY. You mentioned Ingleby's grievance –

MAJOR. Up until then, Mr Ingleby had been the resident photographer in the area.

FRISBY. Up until then?

MAJOR. Up until Hayward's arrival.

FRISBY. Did you ask the Hayward's to leave the town?

MAJOR. On the contrary. Some of the more well to do families in the parish asked me to actively support Hayward's unusual and very popular approach to portraiture – namely photographing people on horses. A splendid idea. Even some of the soldiers in the town were having their photographs taken. They were starting to spend more on photographs than in the pub. No, I was there to ask Hayward to continue the good work. Mr Ingleby would just have to put up with the competition.

FRISBY. Thank you. I must speak to Bert Hill.

THE MAJOR EXITS

ENTER BERT

BERT. Modern science is getting too big for its boots, if you ask me. *(Shakes his hand)* Bert Hill's the name. Did you know, Lewis Hayward's talking of getting some cardboard aeroplanes and photographing people. He reckons air travel is going to be the thing of the future.

FRISBY. Doing something like that would have been guaranteed to annoy Mr Ingleby.

BERT. One more reason for doing it. Mind you, I reckon it's a waste of money.

FRISBY. But enterprise has to be encouraged.

BERT. What about encouraging the poor?

FRISBY. We're living in a century of enormous achievement. Pretty soon we'll have people on the moon.

BERT. And old Lewis Hayward will be there with his camera, I expect.

FRISBY. It'll be recorded on film, that's for sure. These new moving pictures will document the next hundred years, frame by frame.

BERT. Sometimes it's hard keeping up with Lewis. I don't know how his missus can bear it. He's always coming up with new gimmicks.

FRISBY. I understand the business to be doing well. I daresay Lewis Hayward's raking it in while there's money to rake in. One day, it all might disappear.

BERT. Certainly Major White has put a lot of work his way.

FRISBY. It's good having such support from the local community.

BERT. Lewis has his missus to thank for that. I think she's made a big impression on our Major. The man seems smitten. I've never seen the chap so enthusiastic.

FRISBY. I daresay the Major knows a good deal when he sees one.

BERT. People have started talking, you know. The Major's a widower. His wife died three years ago. He has no children.

FRISBY. He's lonely, I expect.

BERT. Lewis needs to be careful. His missus hardly sees him these days. He's always in that studio of his. Now if that was me, my missus would think I was seeing a woman.

FRISBY. *(Looking at Bert)* Somehow, I doubt it.

BERT. I beg your pardon?

FRISBY. Men like Hayward are in love with their work. His camera is his mistress.

BERT. I couldn't say. Now, if you'll excuse me, I've some gardening to attend.

FRISBY. I don't suppose you can shed any light on this card game –

BERT. Sorry. Try speaking to Sarah Hayward – she can shed light on whatever you want.

BERT EXITS

ENTER SARAH

SARAH. Can I help you, Inspector?

FRISBY. I don't think I've had the pleasure.

SARAH. I'm sure you have. But that's neither here or there.

FRISBY. You must be Sarah Hayward.

SARAH. I understand my father's suspected of murdering George Ingleby.

FRISBY. He certainly has a clear motive.

SARAH. I don't think so. My father was doing well in his business. He had no reason to see off George Ingleby. Indeed, annoying Ingleby was becoming a pleasure for my father.

FRISBY. Then who else would have a motive for killing Mr Ingleby?

SARAH. I'm hoping you'll be able to tell me that, Inspector. I'm an avid reader of detective novels – perhaps I could help you solve the crime?

FRISBY. First of all we need a list of suspects. Then we need a motive.

SARAH. Of course, we also need opportunity. Some of our suspects may have alibis.

FRISBY. Mr Ingleby was killed in his studio. Anybody could have done it.

SARAH. You certainly have a wide choice, Inspector.

FRISBY. Then let's start with you, Miss Hayward? Would you have a reason for killing Mr Ingleby?

SARAH. Not at all. I hardly knew the man.

FRISBY. What about your mother?

SARAH. I've known my mother all my life.

FRISBY. I meant – oh, never mind.

SARAH. Have you looked into Mrs Ingleby, Inspector?

FRISBY. Is she worth looking into?

SARAH. If you turn the light down perhaps.

FRISBY. I don't know what you mean.

SARAH. You will find Mrs Ingleby to be a very ambitious woman. Not only was she peeved when my father moved to Aldershot and set up business, she was equally annoyed with her own husband being such a timid competitor. I can say so more.

FRISBY. Why ever not?

SARAH. It's not in my script.

FRISBY. There's more to you than meets the eye. Excuse me, I must speak to Charlie Hill again.

SARAH EXITS

ENTER CHARLIE (CARRYING A PILE OF WOOD)

FRISBY. What are you doing with that lot?

CHARLIE. It's only a bit of wood from the garrisong. I'll get a few shillings for it up the pub.

FRISBY. That wood belongs to the garrison.

CHARLIE. The garrison can spare it.

FRISBY. If you get caught you'll face a heavy fine or fourteen days hard labour.

CHARLIE. I'm not going to get caught. Unless you shop me.

FRISBY. I'm here on a murder investigation. Why don't you get yourself a proper job?

CHARLIE. What sort of work is there around here?

FRISBY. What about farm labouring?

CHARLIE. I'm not suited for farm labouring.

FRISBY. I thought you wanted to join the army. I'm sure the Major would put in a good word for you. There's plenty of regiments garrisoned in the town.

CHARLIE. Gave it up as a bad job.

FRISBY. Then what are you suited for?

CHARLIE. If I knew that, I wouldn't be hanging around the garrison stealing bits of timber.

FRISBY. Tell me, what do you know about Lewis Hayward and his wife?

CHARLIE. Nothing, really. I know Mrs Hayward often goes to London to see theatre shows and what not. She sometimes goes with my mum.

FRISBY. I understand the Major's sweet on Mrs Hayward.

CHARLIE. I couldn't say.

FRISBY. I also understand you're stepping out with Sarah Hayward.

CHARLIE. She's far too interested in her school teaching to bother with the likes of me. I think she's one of these suffering women.

FRISBY. A pity. She would make someone a wonderful wife.

CHARLIE. So, tell me, Inspector. Who do you think killed George Ingleby?

FRISBY. It could be anyone, really.

CHARLIE. My money's on the Major. He's taken with Hayward's wife. He also knows how to handle a gun.

FRISBY. But why kill Ingleby?

CHARLIE. To throw the blame on Lewis Hayward, of course.

FRISBY. Mmmmm. Well, you must excuse me. I must speak to Mrs Ingleby.

CHARLIE EXITS

ENTER MRS INGLEBY

INGLEBY. It's been going on for far too long, Inspector.

FRISBY. It's a free country, Mrs Ingleby. Lewis Hayward can do as he pleases.

INGLEBY. But the Major encourages him.

FRISBY. Your husband should have got himself a few aeroplanes – that would have boosted trade.

INGLEBY. You know my husband wanted to photograph Highview Manor, don't you?

FRISBY. It's certainly a magnificent building. I daresay no self-respecting photographer could trade without a photograph of Highview Manor in his studio.

INGLEBY. The Major refused to allow my husband to photograph Highview Manor.

FRISBY. Let me get this right. Are you saying your husband was being threatened?

INGLEBY. Pressured, more like.

FRISBY. So what did your husband do about it?

INGLEBY. Nothing.

FRISBY. So he let the Major bully him.

INGLEBY. No. Photographing Highview Manor became a passion of my husband. He decided to respect the Major's request. He did not photograph Highview Manor. I did.

FRISBY. You did?

INGLEBY. Why not? I can take a photograph as well as the next man.

FRISBY. That must have infuriated the Major.

INGLEBY. And Mr Hayward.

FRISBY. Giving both men a motive for killing your husband.

INGLEBY. It all fits into place.

FRISBY. Tell me, did the Major or Lewis Hayward know you had photographed Highview Manor?

INGLEBY. They did. I told them both.

FRISBY. Wasn't that rather risky, under the circumstances?

INGLEBY. Who would have thought it would end in murder.

FRISBY. Mrs Ingleby. I really must ask you about this card game –

INGLEBY. It was a friendly game –

FRISBY. *(There is a gunshot Enter Charlie, who dies)* It's Charlie Hill. Quick, help me get him off. We now have two murders to investigate.

THEY EXIT

TWO

ENTER FRISBY AND BERT

FRISBY. I'm afraid your son has been murdered. Shot in the back of the head.

BERT. *(Dazed)* I really don't know what this town is coming to. There's police tramping all over the place. It's bad enough with the army. You can't walk down the pub without bumping into a uniform of one sort or another.

FRISBY. We <u>are</u> investigating two murders, Mr Hill.

BERT. Well, I'll leave you to it then. I'm going for a pint.

FRISBY. You don't seem concerned about your son.

BERT. Charlie could usually be found propping up the bar down the pub. He'll be missed.

FRISBY. He should have got himself a sweetheart.

BERT. He had a sweetheart.

FRISBY. Sarah Hayward didn't want to know.

BERT. Then Charlie should have looked elsewhere. He was a good-looking lad – just like his dad.

FRISBY. But the boy had no prospects. No girl was going to team up with a layabout.

BERT. I never had any prospects when I courted my missus.

FRISBY. I think I rest my case.

BERT. What did you expect me to do about it? I could hardly find the lad a wife.

FRISBY. But you could have got him a job.

BERT. It's hard enough keeping my own job, never mind finding one for Charlie. He should have gone to see that Major pal of Lewis Hayward's. The army's crying out for local lads.

FRISBY. I understand the Major to be more a pal of Mrs Hayward.

BERT. I'm surprised Lewis hasn't put a stop to that. It's the talk of the town, you know.

FRISBY. There's nothing to put a stop to. Mrs Hayward and the Major are just good friends.

BERT. That's not what they say up the pub.

FRISBY. Since when has the Pub been the source of all knowledge?

BERT. What was Charlie doing getting himself shot anyway?

FRISBY. He was found at the back of Ingleby's studio. It appears he was trying to break into Ingleby's shop.

BERT. Who found him?

FRISBY. The Major. Now, I must speak to Sarah Hayward.

BERT EXITS

ENTER SARAH

SARAH. Inspector. What's this about Charlie?

FRISBY. I'm afraid –

SARAH. Charlie and I were such good friends.

FRISBY. I understand he wanted more.

SARAH. He wanted a wife and family. That's not the life for me. I told him that.

FRISBY. I daresay you've too many kiddies around you already, what with your teaching. I daresay it's blunted your natural instincts to have a family of your own.

SARAH. I've seen what having a family can do to people. Women stop being themselves. They become defined by somebody else. They become somebody's wife, somebody's mother –

FRISBY. Somebody's sweetheart.

SARAH. I don't like the way this conversation is going.

FRISBY. Is this how your conversations ended up with Charlie?

SARAH. I just wanted us to be friends.

FRISBY. Men and women can never be friends. There has to be something else.

SARAH. Some men think of nothing else.

FRISBY. I don't blame you for having that opinion. Living around here, amongst so many soldiers – one track minds, I'm afraid.

SARAH. It's not just the soldiers. I've heard stories about girls who go into service. They become fair game for the men of the household – sons and fathers. There's many a young girl who has to leave service for fear of being chased around the bedroom. Some even get themselves caught – if you take my meaning.

FRISBY. Perhaps Charlie should have joined the army. Travelled the world.

SARAH. He could have gone to India. I hear they have servants out in India.

FRISBY. You realise you were leading the lad on, don't you?

SARAH. He asked me several times to marry him, and I turned him down each time. How can that be leading him on?

FRISBY. But you've not taken up with anybody else. That gave the boy hope. The lad thought you were just playing hard to get.

SARAH. So, who killed him, Inspector? And why was he at the back of George Ingleby's shop?

FRISBY. We do have one important clue. (*Frisby shows her a playing card*)

SARAH. But it's just a playing card.

FRISBY. Look at the back – it's marked. Now, I must speak to Annie Hill.

SARAH EXITS

ENTER ANNIE

ANNIE. I wanted my Charlie to get a grip. Do something with his life. He had strong hands and a stronger back. He could work. At the end of the day, that's all any of us can do.

FRISBY. There's more to life than getting a job.

ANNIE. He wanted to join the army. He even went to see the Major about it. But nothing happened. Charlie also had a hankering to travel.

FRISBY. Wouldn't that have broken your heart?

ANNIE. What was there for him in Aldershot? He'd no job to speak of. The pub was his sole source of entertainment.

FRISBY. Where was he thinking of going?

ANNIE. Australia. He said the women there sunbathed every day.

FRISBY. What about work?

ANNIE. There's plenty of sheep.

FRISBY. And if he couldn't get a woman -

ANNIE. He adored Sarah Hayward.

FRISBY. It would appear so.

ANNIE. But she wasn't the one for him. She has ideas above her station, that one.

FRISBY. What do you know about the Hayward family?

ANNIE. Not a lot. I'm friendly enough with Margaret. We go to the shops together sometimes. She likes to spend Lewis' money – been up to London with her a couple of times.

FRISBY. What about Lewis? I hear he spends all his days in his studio.

ANNIE. Comes up with all sorts of fanciful ideas. Spends his time thinking up ways to annoy George Ingleby.

FRISBY. Not any more, he doesn't.

ANNIE. And of course there's the Major. Margaret knows he's sweet on her, but doesn't take advantage of it.

FRISBY. Are you sure about that?

ANNIE. Mind you, there is something about the Hayward family.

FRISBY. Go on.

ANNIE. They came here from Portsmouth. I gather there was a bit of a scandal. I never could get to the bottom of it. But they had to leave in a hurry, by all accounts. My Bert seemed to know more about it – but he can be tight-lipped when he wants to be.

FRISBY. I see. Thank you, Mrs Hill.

ANNIE EXITS

ENTER LEWIS (CARRYING A CAMERA)

FRISBY. Mr Hayward. I'm surprised to see you here.

LEWIS. I've been asked to record the scene of the crime. Forensic evidence, I believe is what they call it.

FRISBY. New-fangled police work.

LEWIS. A bloody sight, all the same. Who would have thought young Charlie to have so many brains?

FRISBY. I daresay you'll turn the photographs into postcards and sell them at tuppence each.

LEWIS. I am a professional, sir. Sixpence is the going rate for something so gruesome.

FRISBY. You haven't seen the Major, have you?

LEWIS. He's busy at the moment.

FRISBY. Perhaps he's with your wife.

LEWIS. What's my wife got to do with anything?

FRISBY. You obviously haven't heard the rumours.

LEWIS. I thought the police dealt in facts, Inspector, not idle gossip.

FRISBY. You spend far too much time in your studio. You look at the world through your lens but you see nothing.

LEWIS. What are you drivelling about?

FRISBY. Your wife and the Major. Even you cannot be so naive.

LEWIS. *(Threatening)* Get away from here, before I do you some serious harm.

FRISBY. You wouldn't get away with something like that.

LEWIS. Oh, really? We've already had two fatalities. Who's to say a local police inspector couldn't make a third? I could even take a photograph of your demise – for posterity.

FRISBY. Tell me, where were you when Mr Ingleby met his maker?

LEWIS. I was in my studio.

FRISBY. Alone?

LEWIS. Of course. Photography is a lonely occupation.

FRISBY. As I'm sure your wife will verify.

LEWIS. And before you ask, I was also in my studio when Charlie Hill met his doom.

FRISBY. How convenient.

LEWIS. The truth often is, Inspector.

FRISBY. I think I need to speak to your wife.

LEWIS EXITS

ENTER MARGARET

MARGARET. That girl of mine's a right little madam. She's going to be the death of me.

FRISBY. Unfortunate choice of words, under the circumstances.

MARGARET. She always has to cross me. It's about time she got herself wed. Go and burden someone else for a change. I don't know why she didn't marry Charlie Hill when she had the chance – put the poor lad out of his misery. *(Realising)* Oh, I'm terribly sorry. I didn't realise.

FRISBY. Perhaps she didn't love him.

MARGARET. What's love got to do with it? And as for that father of hers, he's just as bad.

FRISBY. Your husband can't help it if he has to work. He has a business to run.

MARGARET. He uses his work to escape from his family responsibilities. Especially when it comes to his own daughter.

FRISBY. I daresay it's your own fault. It would appear you brought her up to be independent, filled her head with all this Suffragette nonsense.

MARGARET. She and Charlie Hill had good times together, didn't they? They went to the cinema nearly every week. And what about last summer? That charabanc trip they took to Bournemouth?

FRISBY. I expect she was happy with the way things were. She most probably didn't feel the need to get married and have a husband to tell her what she could and couldn't do.

MARGARET. And she's working too hard in that school of hers. She wants to get out more. Let her hair down. She's become all dowdy.

FRISBY. She's a schoolteacher. She's supposed to be dowdy. Besides, it's satisfying work.

MARGARET. Then she should go up to London on the train. Spend some money in the shops. Get herself some new clothes and scandalise the neighbours. She could even go to a show –

FRISBY. What would Charlie have said?

MARGARET. He would have been shocked.

FRISBY. Don't you have any idea who might have killed Charlie?

MARGARET. He was a bit of fool, but harmless enough.

FRISBY. And what was he doing at the back of Ingleby's shop?

MARGARET. The lad was always up to no good.

FRISBY. Perhaps he was looking for something.

MARGARET. He certainly got more than he bargained for.

FRISBY. We found a playing card in his hand. It was marked.

MARGARET. Unlucky for some.

MARGARET EXITS

ENTER THE MAJOR

MAJOR. Ah, Inspector, I was looking for Margaret.

FRISBY. She's just left.

MAJOR. A pity. There was something I wanted to ask her. I have decided to sell up and move away – once this dreadful mess has been sorted out.

FRISBY. That'll be nice for you.

MAJOR. And I want Margaret to come with me.

FRISBY. I don't understand.

MAJOR. Then I'll make myself clear. Ever since my wife died –

FRISBY. You're lonely, that's all.

MAJOR. I fell in love with Margaret the first day I met her.

FRISBY. Are you really going to destroy your friendship with Margaret?

MAJOR. My wife is dead, I'm about to start a new life and I want her to come with me. Is that so terrible?

FRISBY. In case you hadn't noticed, she's a married woman with a family. Her place is here.

MAJOR. But her husband is never by her side. He neglects her.

FRISBY. He is still her husband.

MAJOR. But I love her.

FRISBY. But does she love you?

MAJOR. Margaret and I are closer than anyone can realise.

FRISBY. I think you had better explain.

MAJOR. She has no feelings for me now, it is true. But it never used to be the case. When she and Lewis lived in Portsmouth –

FRISBY. You knew them in Portsmouth?

MAJOR. I knew Margaret. We used to be – young people have a name for this sort of thing. But her feelings for me died. And when she and Lewis moved here – with a baby girl -

FRISBY. I hope you're not telling me what I think you're telling me.

MAJOR. Not at all! The baby girl belongs to Lewis. But Lewis must never know about Margaret and I. It has to be our secret. Now, please, you must excuse me. I must find Margaret.

FRISBY. Tell me, did George Ingleby know about your secret?

MAJOR. He did.

FRISBY. Which is a perfect motive for murder. Tell me, Major, are you a gambling man?

THE MAJOR EXITS

ENTER BERT

BERT. Those bloody gypsies are at it again. It's about time you lot did something about them.

FRISBY. What is it this time?

BERT. That gypsy encampment in Aldershot. They've started to attack people, you know. On Monday a fight broke out, you lot had to be called in to restore order. The gypsies are nothing but crooks and vagabonds.

FRISBY. The local lads around here are bad enough. Not to mention the soldiers -

BERT. Talking of local lads, any more news on my son's murder?

FRISBY. Nothing, I'm afraid. Nor on the murder of George Ingleby. The chief suspect remains Lewis Hayward. And as for your son's killer -

BERT. Lewis Hayward's too busy to think of anything like that. He's always in that studio of his. Somebody has to make the money to keep that missus of his in finery.

FRISBY. You sound like there's some discord between Mr and Mrs Hayward. Is there anything the matter between them?

BERT. Why should there be anything the matter?

FRISBY. There's talk. Of Mrs Hayward and the Major.

BERT. There's always been talk of Margaret Hayward and the Major. It's nothing but tittle-tattle.

FRISBY. I understand they came here from Portsmouth.

BERT. So?

FRISBY. I just wondered.

BERT. They thought starting a new life would put Portsmouth behind them. And it has. They have a lot to live for here in Aldershot. Sarah is doing well and, like I said, there is nothing between the Major and Margaret Hayward. I promise you. You know what people are like.

FRISBY. Small minds and wicked tongues. I daresay Mrs Hayward's a suffragette.

BERT. These suffragette women are mad, if you ask me – no sense of decency – no sense of reasoning. They're also sexually embittered – lifelong strangers to joy – they want a brood of kids to look after, that'll steady 'em.

FRISBY. Where'd you read that then?

BERT. The Daily Mail. Somebody left a copy in the pub.

FRISBY. If you'll excuse me, I need to speak to Sarah Hayward.

BERT EXITS

ENTER SARAH (CARRYING A TELEGRAM)

SARAH. I've just received this telegram.

FRISBY. Bad news?

SARAH. It's a job offer. From London. They've offered me a teaching post in Islington.

FRISBY. Are you going to take it?

SARAH. I don't know. I suspect I'm needed here in Aldershot.

FRISBY. Do you really want to teach slum kids from London? Not to mention the TB you'd most probably pick up.

SARAH. There's very little to keep me here.

FRISBY. What about your parents?

SARAH. My father's thinking of selling his business – to Mrs Ingleby, of all people.

FRISBY. Are you sure about this? I mean -

SARAH. It's a business proposition. He's not asking her to marry him.

FRISBY. But to sell his business –

SARAH. Mrs Ingleby could just take it. Things would then be as they were before we arrived.

FRISBY. What will your father do?

SARAH. I expect he'll do something else.

FRISBY. Not keep up with photography?

SARAH. He has an itch to make moving pictures. He might go to America and make movies.

FRISBY. And what about Charlie?

SARAH. What about him?

FRISBY. You know he wanted to get matrimonial with you, didn't you?

SARAH. I'm not going to stay here and mooch about something that can now never happen.

FRISBY. Have you no feelings for the lad, at all?

SARAH. He was a friend, nothing more.

FRISBY. To have died without knowing the love of a good woman, that is indeed a tragedy.

SARAH. Who said he died without knowing the love of a good woman?

FRISBY. But I thought –

SARAH. I didn't want to marry the lad – I said nothing about the other. I am a woman, Inspector. I have needs the same as any man. Charlie was more than adequate in that department.

SARAH EXITS. THERE IS A GUNSHOT

ENTER LEWIS

FRISBY. What on earth –

LEWIS. It's the Major. He's shot himself.

FRISBY. But he was fine the last time I saw him.

LEWIS. Was he?

FRISBY. He was talking of leaving. He was looking forward to making a new life for himself. It was going to be a new start for him. Ever since his wife died -

LEWIS. *(Takes out a letter)* He gave this to me. Earlier.

FRISBY. What is it?

LEWIS. It's a goodbye letter.

FRISBY. A suicide note?

LEWIS. Not exactly.

FRISBY. What's it say?

LEWIS. He says he loved my wife.

FRISBY. That was nothing but infatuation on his part.

LEWIS. He says his love was never returned. He envied my having such a loyal and devoted spouse. He says that she gave him no encouragement at all. He is sorry he bothered her with his feelings.

FRISBY. He was a friend. Why does nobody believe that?

LEWIS. She may have been his friend – he wanted more.

FRISBY. How did he die?

LEWIS. He shot himself. They say he was cleaning his gun at the time.

FRISBY. Perhaps they're right to say so, especially if no note was found.

LEWIS. *(Screws up the letter)* Then let's keep his memory untainted.

FRISBY. I understand you're about to sell your business to Mrs Ingleby.

LEWIS. I have already. And I got a good price for it. I've also sold all my equipment to Mrs Ingleby.

FRISBY. A pity. I was hoping you would take my photograph.

LEWIS. You could always go to Mrs Ingleby.

FRISBY. Somehow that would be inappropriate.

LEWIS. One by one, the names are falling off the cast list.

FRISBY. This is not a cheap melodrama, you know. This is real life.

LEWIS EXITS

ENTER MRS INGLEBY

FRISBY. Mrs Ingleby. We need something to move this play on. We're getting bogged down in detail. All these killings. First your husband, then young Charlie and now the Major. There must be a common link.

INGLEBY. There is - Lewis Hayward.

FRISBY. Your husband had a grudge against Hayward – not vica versa. And as for young Charlie Hill -

INGLEBY. Young Charlie carried a torch for Sarah Hayward. Lewis Hayward may have objected to such an attachment.

FRISBY. Feelings that were not returned. Lewis Hayward may have thought Charlie a fool, but Charlie was never a serious contender for Sarah's hand.

INGLEBY. By all accounts, Charlie Hill availed himself of the rest of Sarah Hayward's body – why not her hand also?

FRISBY. You're an evil woman, Mrs Ingleby.

INGLEBY. And what of the Major? His secret association with Margaret Hayward is not as well kept as people suppose.

FRISBY. Are you saying that Lewis Hayward killed the Major because of an earlier association with his wife?

INGLEBY. I'm saying nothing.

FRISBY. There has to be something to spark off this orgy of murder.

INGLEBY. My husband's death happened soon after the card game –

FRISBY. Ah! The famous card game. Will no one tell me the truth about this card game?

INGLEBY. My husband was involved in a card game. In his studio. On the night he died.

FRISBY. Who was at the game?

INGLEBY. I suspect everyone – apart from the women, that is.

FRISBY. What do you mean, everyone?

INGLEBY. My husband. Bert Hill. Charlie. The Major. Lewis Hayward.

FRISBY. Your husband playing cards with Lewis Hayward – isn't that a little strange?

INGLEBY. Not when money is involved. My husband was a good card player. He took great delight in taking money off Lewis Hayward.

FRISBY. *(Takes out the marked card)* Your husband may have been a cheat. Another motive for murder.

INGLEBY. So, someone appears to have finally marked my husband's card.

INGLEBY EXITS

ENTER LEWIS

FRISBY. Perhaps you could shed some light on this famous card game everyone has so conveniently forgotten to tell me about.

LEWIS. George Ingleby was a good card player.

FRISBY. That's a matter of opinion.

LEWIS. Every round we played seemed to end up a head to head with one person. It was as if Ingleby was deliberately playing us off one by one.

FRISBY. Did Ingleby win often?

LEWIS. Almost always.

FRISBY. And did he play a head to head with you on the night he died?

LEWIS. He did. As you've no doubt gathered, Ingleby and I didn't get on. He accused me of taking away his trade.

FRISBY. And beating you at cards was one way of getting back at you.

LEWIS. We played that night. The stakes were high. Everyone was nervous. Then Ingleby had an idea. He wanted the stakes to go even higher, so he devised a game which gambled personal bets.

FRISBY. Personal bets?

LEWIS. He would win all the games. He had all the money and the rest of us had nothing. He would then force us to bet what was most important to us.

FRISBY. And what did you bet?

LEWIS. My business.

FRISBY. And did Ingleby win the game?

LEWIS. He did.

FRISBY. Why did nobody tell me of this win?

LEWIS. Nobody knew. I was to write down my bet on a piece of paper. Only George Ingleby saw the paper. When he won, I walked away. Nobody knew what I had bet.

FRISBY. But you sold your business to Mrs Ingleby.

LEWIS. I did.

FRISBY. But it wasn't yours to sell.

LEWIS. She didn't know that. George Ingleby clearly kept his cards to himself.

FRISBY. So you had a clear motive for killing George Ingleby – to retain your business.

LEWIS. As did all the others at the game. Bert Hill for one.

FRISBY. Thank you, Mr Hayward.

LEWIS EXITS

ENTER BERT

FRISBY. Mr Hill. I understand you were at this card game with George Ingleby.

BERT. Just don't mention it to the missus.

FRISBY. Rather high stakes for a working gardener.

BERT. I just go along for the company – to make up the numbers. I'm usually first out, as it were.

FRISBY. I'm surprised you're allowed in at the start.

BERT. I don't do too bad. I've got a little sideline which keeps me solvent.

FRISBY. Sideline?

BERT. In the woods. The garrison is surrounded by woodland. I've a little brewing business going. I supply the best gargle in the town. George Ingleby is partial to a little drop, as are most of the other men in the card game.

FRISBY. Lewis Hayward tells me of this personal betting that goes on.

BERT. Oh, it goes on, all right. Except on the night in question, it got a bit out of hand.

FRISBY. Did you go head to head with Ingleby?

BERT. I didn't lose much, as it happens. When you ain't got much in the first place –

FRISBY. But you must have bet something of value to Ingleby.

BERT. Information. The currency of the future, if you ask me.

FRISBY. What sort of information?

BERT. Ingleby was always intrigued about the situation between the Major and Margaret Hayward. Like a lot in the town, he wanted to know if there was any fire behind the smoke.

FRISBY. And you played a game of cards on the basis of tittle-tattle?

BERT. Not exactly, no. My bet had to have a little more bite to it.

FRISBY. So what bite were you able to offer?

BERT. Young Sarah.

FRISBY. What about young Sarah?

BERT. The Major and Margaret Hayward did more than exchange glances in Portsmouth, if you take my meaning. Young Sarah Hayward is the result of a very sordid affair.

FRISBY. I don't understand. Your son was sweet on Sarah. Why would you seek to blacken her name in such a way?

BERT. If my lad couldn't have the stuck-up bitch, then nobody would. Feeding Ingleby that juicy titbit would besmirch Sarah Hayward's name in the parish.

FRISBY. Except Ingleby never got chance to use the information.

BERT. No, someone got to him first.

BERT EXITS

ENTER MARGARET

MARGARET. Was that Bert Hill I saw?

FRISBY. It was.

MARGARET. Spreading tittle-tattle, I expect.

FRISBY. Why do you say that?

MARGARET. Because the man has nothing better to do with his time. He's up to all sorts of tricks, you know. And he drinks.

FRISBY. You've obviously heard of this game of cards George Ingleby was involved in.

MARGARET. Men and their gambling. If they're not drinking, they're playing cards.

FRISBY. Quite an eventful game, from all accounts.

MARGARET. I'm just glad Lewis doesn't get involved in that sort of thing.

FRISBY. So you know nothing of the game on the night George Ingleby died?

MARGARET. I knew there was a game, yes.

FRISBY. Did you know the stakes were higher than usual? Secret bets being placed.

MARGARET. Secret bets?

FRISBY. You and the Major –

MARGARET. Please don't bring that up again. The poor man deserves to rest in peace.

FRISBY. I understand you knew the Major in Portsmouth.

MARGARET. Who told you that?

FRISBY. I understand you knew him extremely well.

MARGARET. How could you know something like that? George Ingleby is dead –

FRISBY. Who told you that George Ingleby knew about you and the Major?

MARGARET. Nobody.

FRISBY. Was it the Major? Was Ingleby trying to blackmail the Major? Is that why the Major killed himself?

MARGARET. The Major killed himself because of that stupid card game. The Major bet Highview Manor – and lost. Ingleby knew about the Major and I. He put that knowledge on the table. Everyone's happiness depended on a turn of a card.

FRISBY. And now the Major is dead – as is George Ingleby.

MARGARET. I don't know how George Ingleby knew about me and the Major in the first place. We covered our tracks well.

FRISBY. You were looking for Bert Hill, I believe.

MARGARET EXITS

ENTER ANNIE

ANNIE. You haven't seen my Bert, have you?

FRISBY. He was here a moment ago.

ANNIE. I expect he's gone into the woods. He spends so much time there - he must have a lady love.

FRISBY. Aren't you worried by that?

ANNIE. Not a bit of it. If he has got someone else, then good luck to him. It saves him bothering me, don't it?

FRISBY. Do you and Bert not get on then?

ANNIE. Oh, we get on, all right. It's getting the bugger off that I want. I don't know where he gets the lead for his pencil from. I'll tell you what, it must be the bark in them trees. My Bert goes into the woods and comes out a changed man. Whatever he's got in there, needs to be bottled.

FRISBY. I don't suppose you know anything about this card game that George Ingleby ran on the night he died?

ANNIE. Know about it, we all knew about it. Ingleby tried to keep it a secret, but the whole world knew.

FRISBY. So you didn't mind your Bert going?

ANNIE. My Bert ain't no good at cards and ain't no good at gambling. Bert's just there to make the numbers up and get the drinks in when everyone else is getting excited.

FRISBY. It's a pity the women can't play – it might stop the men from losing their heads.

ANNIE. Who says the women don't play?

FRISBY. I thought it was men only.

ANNIE. Most times it is, yes. But not on the night George Ingleby drew his last hand.

FRISBY. Are you telling me there were women at that game?

ANNIE. Our Charlie took the Hayward girl – Sarah.

FRISBY. Sarah Hayward was at the card game?

ANNIE. I daresay he wanted to impress her – it'll take more than a card game to impress that one, I can tell you.

FRISBY. I understand there were head to head sessions with George Ingleby.

ANNIE. There usually was to my reckoning.

FRISBY. Did Charlie go head to head with Ingleby?

ANNIE. You better ask Sarah Hayward that question?

ANNIE EXITS

ENTER SARAH

FRISBY. I understand you were at the card game on the night George Ingleby died.

SARAH. I was. Charlie took me.

FRISBY. Did you play?

SARAH. I mainly watched Charlie.

FRISBY. Did Charlie play well?

SARAH. No worse than the rest of them.

FRISBY. Do you know of this secret betting that went on?

SARAH. I did.

FRISBY. Did Charlie place a secret bet?

SARAH. Charlie's got nothing to bet. He's not exactly a man of property.

FRISBY. So Charlie didn't go head to head with Ingleby.

SARAH. I didn't say that.

FRISBY. I don't understand. If Charlie had nothing to bet –

SARAH. But I did. The secret betting is easy. You simply write down what you want to bet, hand it to your opponent, if he (or she) agrees to the bet, then the game continues.

FRISBY. What did you bet?

SARAH. That's the whole point – it's a secret.

FRISBY. Did Charlie know what you bet?

SARAH. Like I said – it's a secret.

FRISBY. Let me get this right. Charlie went into head to head with George Ingleby. The lad had nothing to bet and was about to quit the game –

SARAH. When I stepped in.

FRISBY. I have to tell you that this is a police investigation. I suspect that your secret bet is important evidence.

SARAH. Inspector, can't you guess what I bet?

FRISBY. The only thing you have to bet is – yourself.

SARAH. Precisely!

FRISBY. What! George Ingleby won you in a game of cards?

SARAH. You shouldn't look so shocked, Inspector. Now, if you'll excuse me.

SARAH EXITS

ENTER MARGARET

FRISBY. Ah, Mrs Hayward. I was just thinking of you.

MARGARET. Are you any nearer to solving the crime?

FRISBY. Of course we mustn't forget – there have been three deaths.

MARGARET. Do you think they are connected?

FRISBY. Possibly.

MARGARET. If I can be of any assistance –

FRISBY. You are an intelligent woman. Perhaps I can bounce the evidence off you. Just to clarify matters in my own mind.

MARGARET. Bounce away, Inspector.

FRISBY. George Ingleby has been murdered. So far so good – although not for him. We know about this card game he was involved in and we know matters were getting out of hand. We also know that secret bets were being placed – bets which may well have led to murder.

MARGARET. Or murders.

FRISBY. May I be frank with you, Mrs Hayward?

MARGARET. I thought your name was Frisby?

FRISBY. George Ingleby was an unpleasant man. Your husband bet his business that fateful night.

MARGARET. If that was true, why did he sell it to Mrs Ingleby?

FRISBY. We also know that Bert Hill bet an embarrassing secret.

MARGARET. What he does in the woods is his own concern.

FRISBY. Bert Hill knew about you and the Major.

MARGARET. Bert Hill knew nothing.

FRISBY. He also knew about Sarah being the Major's daughter.

MARGARET. The Major and I made a terrible mistake. It was a long time ago.

FRISBY. Talking of the Major, did you know he bet Highview Manor – and lost?

MARGARET. Sarah has nothing to do with this dreadful business, you know.

FRISBY. That's where you're wrong. Sarah was with Charlie at the card game. Charlie had nothing to bet – but Sarah had. She is a modern young woman.

MARGARET. Are you telling me Sarah placed her own virtue on the card table?

FRISBY. An evocative thought, I must admit.

MARGARET EXITS

ENTER ANNIE

ANNIE. Are you still here, Inspector?

FRISBY. Why wouldn't I be here?

ANNIE. It's almost time to go home.

FRISBY. Nobody's going home just yet. We have murders to solve.

ANNIE. You ain't doing much of a job, are you?

FRISBY. Aren't you concerned? Your own son has lost his life.

ANNIE. To tell you the truth, my Charlie was a bit of dead loss. He never made much of his life when he was around – I don't expect him to make much of his death now he's gone.

FRISBY. That's a bit harsh.

ANNIE. He had no pride. He let that Hayward girl run rings around him. She humiliated the boy.

FRISBY. I can see she's a spirited enough girl –

ANNIE. She's a loose woman, that's what she is. I could tell you stories –

FRISBY. Please, go ahead.

ANNIE. For a start, she's not of Lewis Hayward's loins – you just ask my Bert.

FRISBY. And?

ANNIE. And she offered her favours to all and sundry.

FRISBY. On the night of George Ingleby's death perhaps?

ANNIE. You know about that? Fancy giving up your cherry over a game of cards?

FRISBY. I think her cherry gave up the ghost some time ago.

ANNIE. Wouldn't surprise me. Anyway, like I said. Time to depart. Some of us have beds to go to.

FRISBY. Nobody can leave until we solve the murders.

ANNIE.. Who do you think is the murderer, Inspector? My money's on that Mrs Ingleby – a vindictive little cow, if you ask me.

ANNIE EXITS

ENTER MRS INGLEBY

INGLEBY. Who's a vindictive little cow?

FRISBY. Strange, you buying Hayward's business off him.

INGLEBY. Strange him selling it.

FRISBY. Perhaps it wasn't his to sell.

INGLEBY. I don't get you.

FRISBY. Lewis Hayward has a wicked sense of humour. Selling his business to a woman who already owned it would have tickled his funny bone.

INGLEBY. I don't understand you.

FRISBY. The card game. Your husband won Hayward's photography business off him.

INGLEBY. If he did, it's news to me.

FRISBY. And the Major – did you not know about his loss?

INGLEBY. What loss?

FRISBY. Your husband won Highview Manor on the night he died.

INGLEBY. I don't believe this.

FRISBY. It was a lucky night for your husband – he also won the fair hand of Sarah Hayward.

INGLEBY. Are you telling me my husband and that strumpet –

FRISBY. Mind you, that fateful card game was unlucky for some. Lewis Hayward lost his livelihood and the Major lost his life – and as for young Charlie –

INGLEBY. Perhaps Charlie saw what he shouldn't have seen.

FRISBY. For instance?

INGLEBY. If my husband was with young Sarah Hayward – and if Charlie was witness to the carnal deed –

FRISBY. Are you saying Charlie killed your husband – in a fit of jealous rage?

INGLEBY. I'm saying nothing.

FRISBY. Why ever not?

INGLEBY. It's not in my script.

FRISBY. Never mind the script. *(To the audience)* Ladies and gentlemen. We have attempted to solve the various murders this evening to no avail. However, we do know the following - George Ingleby has been murdered. All the chief suspects were involved in a card game on the night of the killing. Lewis Hayward lost his business in that card game. The Major lost Highview Manor in the same game – not to mention his life. Bert Hill lost nothing except the information relating to the Major and Mrs Hayward. Charlie Hill lost nothing that night except the woman he loved – and his life of course. Sarah Hayward lost that which had vanished a long time ago.

ENTER LEWIS (CARRRYING HIS CAMERA)

LEWIS. Inspector, would it be possible to take a picture of all the main participants this evening? This is such an intriguing crime, it's bound to enter the annals of unsolved murders.

FRISBY. We still might solve the murder.

LEWIS. In the meantime, can I take my photograph?

FRISBY. By all means, who do you need?

LEWIS. I think Annie and Bert Hill for a start. *(Enter Annie and Bert)*

FRISBY. Who else?

LEWIS. I think my darling wife – not to mention my dear daughter, Sarah. *(Enter Margaret and Sarah)*

FRISBY. Anyone else?

LEWIS. I daresay I better have Mrs Ingleby in the picture. After all, it is her camera I'm using. *(Enter Mrs Ingleby)*

FRISBY. I think that's all we can have at the moment – unless there is some way of raising the dead.

LEWIS. One day, photography will be so exact that images of dead people can be grafted onto the bodies of living being.

FRISBY. Rather like your idea of placing heads on horses and bodies in aeroplanes.

LEWIS. Precisely! Now for the picture.

FRISBY. Please, allow me to assist. I see you haven't got a photographic plate in the camera.

LEWIS. So I haven't.

FRISBY. You have some in this box, I see. *(Frisby rumages in a nearby box. He takes out some photographs)* Ah, what do we have here? Photographs of your dear wife – with nothing to cover her modesty.

LEWIS. Those photographs are mine.

FRISBY. They are also explicit.

LEWIS. Taken in a private capacity.

FRISBY. Here's one of Mrs Ingleby also. A candid view of her bathing.

LEWIS. That's not one of mine.

FRISBY. It's not, is it? This is one that George Ingleby has taken. And here, one of Mrs Hill – equally saucy. So, she does show her private bits to the world. And here, one of Sarah Hayward – who says gambling doesn't pay.

LEWIS. These are all artistic photographs for discerning customers.

FRISBY. Such as billotted soldiers in the army barracks hereabouts – men away from their loved ones – men who will pay a shilling a piece for images such as these.

LEWIS. You have nothing on me. These all belong to George Ingleby. And Ingleby is not around to say different.

FRISBY. No, but the Major is – *(Enter the Major)*

LEWIS. What on earth are you doing here?

FRISBY. Not to mention young Charlie Hill. *(Enter Charlie)*

LEWIS. I don't understand any of this.

FRISBY. It's easy. The Major and Charlie have been working together. The army contacted the Major to see if could help with this traffic in filth. The Major suspected you – and Ingleby - of working in cahoots and decided to set a trap for you both. He was unable to work alone so he enlisted young Charlie to help. Charlie always wanted to be in the army, this was his golden opportunity.

LEWIS. But both of them are dead.

FRISBY. Trickery, fakery and fraud. They both feigned death to go underground. It soon became clear that you were hiding the plates under your floorboards – we needed time to excavate the evidence.

LEWIS. You have no proof.

FRISBY. George Ingleby wanted a bigger share of the profits. You discovered he had been cheating. You also discovered that he had won your own daughter's hand. Unlucky for some, eh?

LEWIS. At least allow me to take my photograph.

FRISBY. It's the least I can do. It will give all these good people chance to take a bow and soak in the applause of the audience.

THEY LINE UP FOR A PHOTOGRAPH

END OF PLAY

Printed in Great Britain
by Amazon

42209753R00067